GERMAN
PHRASEBOOK

**GEDDES &
GROSSET**

Published 2006 by Geddes & Grosset,
David Dale House, New Lanark, ML11 9DJ, Scotland

© 1998 Geddes & Grosset

First published 1998
Reprinted 1999, 2000, 2001, 2002, 2003, 2004, 2005, 2006

ISBN 10: 1 85534 345 2
ISBN 13: 978 1 85534 345 0

Printed and bound in Poland

POLSKABOOK

CONTENTS

4

CONTENTS

CONTENTS

8

KEY TO PRONUNCIATION

Guide to German pronunciation scheme

Vowels

a	as in bad, father
e	as in bed, father
ee	as in see
i	as in bit
y	as in bite
o	as in hot
oa	as in boat
w	as in fowl
oo	as in pool
û	as in French tu

Consonants have approximately the same sounds as in English, but note the following:

g	as in get
kh	as in the German name Bach, Scottish loch
zh	as in measure

GETTING STARTED

Everyday words and phrases

Yes
Ja
ya

Yes, please
Ja bitte
ya bit-e

No
Nein
nyn

No, thank you
Nein danke
nyn dank-e

OK
In Ordnung
*in **ord**-noong*

Please
Bitte
***bit**-e*

Thank you
Danke
***dank**-e*

Excuse me
Entschuldigung
*ent-**shool**-ee-goong*

Good
Gut
goot

I am very sorry
Es tut mir sehr leid
*es **toot** meer zayr **lyt***

Being understood

I do not speak German
Ich spreche kein Deutsch
*eekh **shprekh**-e kyn **doytsh***

I do not understand
Ich verstehe nicht
*eekh fer-**shtay**-e neekht*

Can you find someone who speaks English?
Könnten Sie jemanden finden, der Englisch spricht?
*koent-en zee yay-mand-en **find**-en der **eng**-leesh shprikht*

Can you help me, please?
Können Sie mir bitte helfen?
*koen-en zee meer **bit**-e **help**-en*

It does not matter
Keine Ursache
*kyn-e **oor**-zakh-e*

I do not mind
Macht nichts
makht neekhts

Please repeat that slowly
Bitte wiederholen Sie das langsam
*bit-e veed-er-**hoal**-en zee das **lang**-zam*

12

Greetings and exchanges

Hello
Hallo
ha-loa

Hi
Hallo
ha-loa

Good evening
Guten Abend
goot-en a-bent

Good morning
Guten Morgen
goot-en mor-gen

Good night
Gute Nacht
goot-e nakht

Goodbye
Auf Wiedersehen
owf veed-er-zay-en

How are you?
Wie geht es Ihnen?
vee gayt es een-en

Greetings and exchanges

I am very well, thank you
Danke, es geht mir sehr gut
dank-e es gayt meer zayr goot

It is good to see you
Schön, Sie zu sehen
shoen zee tsoo zay-en

It is nice to meet you
Angenehm, Ihre Bekanntschaft zu machen
an-ge-naym eer-e be-kannt-shaft tsoo makh-en

There are five of us
Wir sind zu fünft
veer zint tsoo fûnft

Here is my son
Hier ist mein Sohn
heer ist myn zoan

This is — my daughter
Das ist — meine Tochter
das ist — myn-e tokht-er

    — my husband
    — mein Mann
    — myn man

    — my wife
    — meine Frau
    — myn-e frow

My name is . . .
Mein Name ist . . .
*myn **nam**-e ist . . .*

What is your name?
Was ist Ihr Name?
*vas ist eer **nam**-e*

You are very kind
Sehr nett von Ihnen
*zayr **net** fon **een**-en*

You are very welcome!
Bitte sehr
***bit**-e zayr*

See you soon
Bis bald
*bis **balt***

I am on holiday
Ich bin auf Urlaub
*eekh bin owf **oor**-lowp*

I live in London
Ich wohne in London
*eekh **voan**-e in **lon**-don*

I am a student
Ich bin Student
*eekh bin shtoo-**dent***

Greetings and exchanges

I am from America
Ich komme aus Amerika
*eekh **kom**-e ows a-**may**-ree-ka*

   I am from — Australia
Ich komme aus — Australien
*eekh **kom**-e ows — ow-**stra**-lee-en*

      — Britain
      — Großbritannien
      *— **groas**-bri-**ta**-nee-en*

      — Canada
      — Kanada
      *— **ka**-na-da*

      — England
      — England
      *— **eng**-lant*

      — Ireland
      — Irland
      *— **eer**-lant*

      — New Zealand
      — Neuseeland
      *— noy-**zay**-lant*

      — Scotland
      — Schottland
      *— **shot**-lant*

— **South Africa**
— Südafrika
— *zûd-af-ree-ka*

— **Wales**
— Wales
— *wayls*

Common questions

Where?	**How?**
Wo?	Wie?
voa	*vee*
Where is...?	**How much?**
Wo ist...?	Wieviel
voa ist	*vee-feel*
Where are...?	**Who?**
Wo sind...?	Wer?
voa zint	*vayr*
When?	**Why?**
Wann?	Warum?
van	*va-room*
What?	**Which?**
Was?	Welcher / Welche / Welches
vas	*velkh-er / velkh-e / velkh-es*

Common questions

Do you know a good restaurant?
Kennen Sie ein gutes Restaurant?
*ken-en zee yn **goot**-es rest-oa-**rong***

How can I contact American Express / Diners Club?
Wie kann ich mich mit American Express / dem Diners
  Club in Verbindung setzen?
*vee kan eekh meekh mit A-**mer**-ican Express / dem **Dyn**-ers
  Club in fer-**bind**-oong **zets**-en*

Do you mind if I . . .
Stört es Sie, wenn ich . . .
***stoert** es zee ven eekh . . .*

Have you got any change?
Können Sie wechseln?
***koen**-en zee **veks**-eln*

How long will it take?
Wie lange dauert das?
*vee **lang**-e **dow**-ert das*

May I borrow your map?
Darf ich Ihre Karte borgen?
***darf** eekh eer-e **kart**-e borg-en*

What is the problem?
Was ist das Problem
*vas ist das prob-**laym***

What is this?
Was ist das?
*vas ist **das***

What is wrong?
Was ist nicht in Ordnung? / Was ist los?
*vas ist **neekht** in **ord**-noong / vas ist **loas***

What time do you close?
Wann schließen Sie?
*van **shlees**-en zee*

Where can I buy a postcard?
Wo kann ich eine Postkarte kaufen?
***voa** kan eekh yn-e **post**-kart-e **kowf**-en*

Where can I change my clothes?
Wo kann ich mich umziehen?
***voa** kan eekh meekh **oom**-tsee-en*

Where can we sit down?
Wo können wir uns hinsetzen?
***voa** koen-en veer oons **hin**-zets-en*

Who did this?
Wer hat das getan?
vayr** hat das ge-**tan

Who should I see about this?
Mit wem müßte ich darüber sprechen?
*mit **vaym** mûst-e eekh da-**rûb**-er **shprekh**-en*

Asking the time

Will you come?
Kommen Sie?
kom-en zee

Asking the time

What time is it?
Wieviel Uhr ist es?
*vee-feel **oor** ist es*

It is —
Es ist —
es ist —

> **— a quarter past ten**
> — viertel elf / viertel nach zehn
> — *feer-tel **elf** / feer-tel nakh **tsayn***

> **— a quarter to eleven**
> — viertel vor elf / dreiviertel elf
> — *feer-tel foar **elf** / dry-veer-tel **elf***

> **— after three o'clock**
> — nach drei Uhr
> — *nakh **dry** oor*

> **— early**
> — früh
> — *frû*

20

Asking the time

— **eleven o'clock**
— elf Uhr
— *elf oor*

— **five past ten**
— fünf nach zehn
— *fûnf nakh tsayn*

— **five to eleven**
— fünf vor elf
— *fûnf foar elf*

— **half past eight exactly**
— genau halb neun
— *ge-now halp noyn*

— **half past ten**
— halb elf
— *halp elf*

— **late**
— spät
— *spet*

— **midnight**
— Mitternacht
— *mit-er-nakht*

— **nearly five o'clock**
— fast fünf Uhr
— *fast fûnf oor*

Asking the time

— ten o' clock
— zehn Uhr
— *tsayn oor*

— ten past ten
— zehn nach zehn
— *tsayn nakh **tsayn***

— ten to eleven
— zehn vor elf
— *tsayn foar **elf***

— twelve o'clock (midday)
— zwölf Uhr (Mittag)
— *tsvoelf oor (**mi**-tag)*

— twenty-five past ten
— fünfundzwanzig Minuten nach zehn
— *fûnf-oont-**tsvan**-tseekh mee-**noo**-ten nakh **tsayn***

— twenty-five to eleven
— fünfundzwanzig Minuten vor elf
— *fûnf-oont-**tsvan**-tseekh mee-**noo**-ten voar **elf***

— twenty past ten
— zwanzig Minuten nach zehn
— ***tsvan**-tseekh mee-**noo**-ten nakh **tsayn***

— twenty to eleven
— zwanzig Minuten vor elf
— ***tsvan**-tseekh mee-**noo**-ten foar **elf***

22

Common problems

at about one o'clock
etwa um ein Uhr
*et-va oom **yn** oor*

soon
bald
balt

at half past six
um halb sieben
*oom halp **zeeb**-en*

this afternoon
heute Nachmittag
*hoyt-e **nakh**-mi-tag*

at night
nachts
nakhts

this evening
heute Abend
*hoyt-e **a**-bent*

before midnight
vor Mitternacht
*foar **mit**-er-nakht*

this morning
heute morgen
*hoyt-e **mor**-gen*

in an hour's time
in einer Stunde
*in yn-er **shtoond**-e*

tonight
heute nacht
*hoyt-e **nakht***

in half an hour
in einer halben Stunde
*in yn-er halb-en **shtoond**-e*

two hours ago
vor zwei Stunden
*foar tsvy **shtoond**-en*

Common problems

I am late
Ich bin schon zu spät
*eekh bin **shoan** tsoo **shpet***

Common problems

I have dropped a contact lens
Mir ist eine Kontaktlinse heruntergefallen
*meer ist yn-e kon-**takt**-linz-e hayr-**oont**-er-ge-fal-en*

I have no currency
Ich habe nicht die richtige Währung
*eekh **hab**-e neekht dee **reekht**-eeg-e **ver**-oong*

I haven't enough money
Ich habe nicht genug Geld
*eekh **hab**-e **neekht** ge-**noog** gelt*

I have lost my — credit cards
Ich habe meine — Kreditkarten verloren
*eekh **hab**-e myn-e — kray-**deet**-kart-en fer-**loar**-en*

— **key**
— Schlüssel verloren
— *shlûs-el fer-**loar**-en*

— **ticket**
— Karte verloren
— *kart-e fer-**loar**-en*

— **traveller's cheques**
— Reiseschecks verloren
— *ryz-e-sheks fer-**loar**-en*

My car has been stolen
Mein Wagen wurde gestohlen
*myn **vag**-en voord-e ge-**shtoal**-en*

24

My handbag has been stolen
Meine Handtasche wurde gestohlen
*myn-e **hant**-tash-e voord-e ge-**shtoal**-en*

My wallet has been stolen
Mein Geldbeutel wurde gestohlen
*myn **gelt**-boyt-el voord-e ge-**shtoal**-en*

My son is lost
Ich habe meinen Sohn verloren
*eekh **hab**-e myn-en **zoan** fer-**loar**-en*

ARRIVING IN GERMANY

By air

The major airlines operating from the UK to Germany are British Airways, Lufthansa and Air UK, which offer regular daily departures. There are also low cost alternatives with a limited number of flights.

International airports are situated at Berlin, Bremen, Dusseldorf, Dresden, Frankfurt on Main, Hamburg, Hannover, Cologne/Bonn, Leipzig, Munich, Münster/Osnabrück, Nuremberg, Stuttgart and Saarbrücken. All airports have quick and easy links to the road network of a given city and Lufthansa offers a train service for air ticket holders between Cologne and Frankfurt. Frankfurt has the biggest airport in Europe, which is linked to the InterCity rail network by a station under the terminal.

For cheap flights on major airlines look into APEX or Super-APEX ticket options, which should be booked in advance and have certain restrictions.

Germany's internal air network is excellent, and it is possible to travel from north to south or from east to west in little over an hour. Services are operated by Deutsche BA, Lufthansa and LTU. In addition, smaller airlines offer a limited service to the North Frisian Islands.

By ferry

The following companies operate car ferries from the UK: Sealink, Eurolink Ferries, P&O European Ferries, North Sea Ferries, and Motorail. The only direct ferry link from the UK to Germany goes to Hamburg. Other popular connections are from Dover, Ramsgate, Harwich, Hull and Newcastle to Calais, Ostende, Rotterdam, Zeebrugge or Esbjerg.

By train

There are several ways to reach Germany from London by rail. Travellers may take the Channel Tunnel to save time, leaving London on the Eurostar hourly from Waterloo. To proceed to Germany they would have to change trains in Brussels. Much cheaper and slower are the regular departures from Victoria using the Ramsgate-Ostend ferry, Jetfoil or SeaCat service.

By coach

There are three departures a day from London's Victoria Coach Station. The buses cross the channel on Sealink's Dover-Zeebrugge ferry service and then drive via the Netherlands and Belgium to Cologne, Frankfurt, Mannheim, Stuttgart/Nurnberg, and Munich. Hoverspeed runs buses from Victoria Station to Berlin.

Arrival

Here is my passport
Da ist mein Paß
da ist myn pas

I am attending a convention
Ich wohne einer Versammlung bei
eekh voan-e yn-er fer-zam-loong by

I am here on business
Ich bin geschäftlich hier
eekh bin ge-sheft-leekh heer

I will be staying here for eight weeks
Ich bleibe acht Wochen lang hier
eekh blyb-e akht vokh-en lang heer

We are visiting friends
Wir besuchen Freunde
veer be-zookh-en froynd-e

We have a joint passport
Wir haben einen Sammelpaß
veer hab-en yn-en zam-el-pas

I have nothing to declare
Ich habe nichts anzumelden
eekh hab-e neekhts an-tsoo-meld-en

I have the usual allowances
Ich habe die üblichen zollfrei erlaubten Mengen
*eekh **hab**-e dee **ûb**-leekh-en **tsol**-fry er-lowp-ten **meng**-en*

How long will this take?
Wie lange dauert das?
*vee **lang**-e **dow**-ert das*

How much do I have to pay?
Was habe ich zu zahlen?
***vas** hab-e eekh tsoo **tsal**-en*

This is for my own use
Das ist für meinen eigenen Gebrauch
das** ist fûr myn-en **yg**-en-en ge-**browkh

Common problems and requests

Can I upgrade to first class?
Kann ich ein Upgrade zur ersten Klasse haben?
***kan** eekh yn **up**-grayd tsoor **erst**-en klas-e **hab**-en*

How long will the delay be?
Wie groß ist die Verspätung?
*vee **groas** ist dee fer-**spet**-oong*

I am in a hurry
Ich bin in Eile
*eekh bin in **yl**-e*

Common problems and requests

I have lost my ticket
Ich habe mein Ticket verloren
eekh hab-e myn tik-et fer-loar-en

I have missed my connection
Ich habe meinen Anschluß verpaßt
eekh hab-e myn-en an-shloos fer-past

The people who were to meet me have not arrived
Die Leute, die mich abholen sollten, sind nicht
  angekommen
*dee loyt-e dee meekh ap-hoal-en zolt-en zint neekht
  an-ge-kom-en*

Where is the toilet?
Wo finde ich eine Toilette?
voa find-e eekh eyn-e toy-let-e

Where is — the bar?
  Wo ist — die Bar?
  voa ist — dee bar

    — the information desk?
    — der Informationsschalter?
    — der in-for-ma-tsee-oans-shalt-er

    — the departure lounge?
    — der Wartesaal?
    — voa ist der vart-e-zal

30

Common problems and requests

— the transfer desk?
— der Transfer-Schalter
— *der trans-fer-shalt-er*

Where can I buy currency?
Wo kann ich Landeswährung kaufen?
voa kan eekh land-ez-ver-oong kowf-en

Where can I change traveller's cheques?
Wo kann ich meine Reiseschecks umwechseln?
voa kan eekh myn-e ryz-e-sheks oom-veks-eln

Where can I get a taxi?
Wo kann ich ein Taxi nehmen?
voa kan eekh yn tax-ee naym-en

Where do I get the connection flight to Cologne?
Wo finde ich einen Anschlußflug nach Köln?
voa find-e eekh yn-en an-shloos-floog nakh koeln

Where will I find the airline representative?
Wo finde ich einen Vertreter der Fluggesellschaft?
voa find-e eekh yn-en fer-trayt-er der floog-ge-zel-shaft

My flight was late
Mein Flug hat sich verspätet
myn floog hat zeekh fer-shpet-et

I was delayed at the airport
Ich wurde am Flughafen aufgehalten
eekh woord-e am floog-haf-en owf-ge-halt-en

Luggage

I was held up at immigration
Ich wurde bei den Einwanderungsbehörden aufgehalten
*eekh woord-e by den **yn**-vand-er-oongs-be-**hoerd**-en owf-gehalt-en*

Luggage

Where is the baggage from flight number...?
Wo ist das Gepäck von Flug Nummer...?
*voa ist das ge-**pek** fon **floog noom**-er...*

Are there any baggage trolleys?
Gibt es hier Gepäckwagen?
*gipt es heer ge-**pek**-vag-en*

Can I have help with my bag?
Könnte mir jemand mit meiner Tasche helfen?
*koent-e meer yay-mant mit myn-er **tash**-e helf-en*

Careful, the handle is broken
Achtung, der Griff ist kaputt
*akh-toong der **grif** ist ka-**poot***

I will carry that myself
Das trage ich selbst
*das **trag**-e eekh **zelpst***

Is there a left-luggage office?
Gibt es hier eine Gepäckverwarung?
*gipt es **heer** yn-e ge-**pek**-fer-**var**-oong*

Is there any charge?
Kostet das etwas?
kost-et das et-vas

Where is my bag?
Wo ist meine Tasche?
voa ist myn-e tash-e

I have lost my bag
Ich habe meine Tasche verloren
eekh hab-e myn-e tash-e fer-loar-en

It is — a large suitcase
Es ist — ein großer Koffer
es ist — yn gros-er kof-er

— a rucksack
— ein Rucksack
— *yn rook-zak*

— a small bag
— eine kleine Tasche
— *yn-e klyn-e tash-e*

My baggage has not arrived
Mein Gepäck ist nicht angekommen
myn ge-pek ist neekht an-ge-kom-en

Please take these bags to a taxi
Bitte bringen Sie diese Taschen in ein Taxi
bit-e bring-en zee deez-e tash-en in yn tax-ee

Luggage

These bags are not mine
Das ist nicht mein Gepäck
*das ist **neekht** myn ge-**pek***

This package is fragile
Dieses Paket ist zerbrechlich
*deez-es pa-**kayt** ist tser-**brekh**-leekh*

No, do not put that on top
Nein, stellen Sie das bitte nicht darauf
nyn shtel**-en zee das **bit**-e neekht da-**rowf

34

AT THE HOTEL

Types of Hotel

The standard of German hotels is very high. There are great variations in prices, and although there is no official grading system for German hotels, you are usually welcomed politely and courteously and given polite service. Rooms are clean and comfortable and breakfast is usually included. It is worth asking for non-smoking rooms in larger hotels.

If you are looking for a guest house or B & B, there are many *Gasthöfe* or *Gasthäuser,* country inns offering food and rooms, *Fremdenheime* or *Pensionen* (guest houses), with *Fremdenzimmer,* which are rooms in private houses, at the lowest end of the scale. The words *Zimmer frei* or *zu vermieten* on a green background means there are vacancies while *besetzt*, on a red background, means no vacancies.

Most hotels have restaurants but those listed as *Garni* provide breakfast only. Lists of German hotels are available from the German National Tourist Office, 65 Curzon Street, London W1Y 8NE.

Castle Hotels

Germany's castle, or *Schloss,* hotels are of considerable interest. They are privately owned and run, and the majority

Types of Hotel

offer four star luxury combined with the atmosphere of antique furnishings and stone passageways. For a brochure listing these hotels, write to Gast im Schloss e.V., D-34388 Trendelburg.

Romantik Hotels

These are of similar interest to castle hotels, being privately run in historic buildings with an emphasis on excellent food.

Spas

Taking the waters in Germany has been popular since Roman times. There are over 300 health resorts and mineral springs in the country. The word 'Bad' at the beginning of a place name usually indicates a spa, offering treatment at fairly high prices. Although there are spas in eastern Germany, most are in need of renovation. For information, write to Deutscher Bäderverband e.V., Schumannstr. 111, D-53113 Bonn.

Farm holidays

More and more holiday makers are opting for a holiday on a farm (*Urlaub auf dem Bauernhof*). Brochure listings are available from local tourist offices or from DLG Verlags GmbH, Eschenheimer Landstrasse 122, D-60489 Frankfurt am Main.

Reservations and enquiries

I am sorry I am late
Bitte entschuldigen Sie die Verspätung
bit-e ent-shoold-eeg-en zee dee fer-shpet-oong

I have a reservation
Ich habe gebucht
eekh hab-e ge-bookht

I shall be staying until July 4th
Ich werde bis vierten Juli bleiben
eekh vayrd-e bis feer-ten yool-ee blyb-en

I want to stay for 5 nights
Ich möchte fünfmal übernachten
eekh moekht-e fûnf-mal û-ber-nakht-en

Do you have a double room with a bath?
Haben Sie ein Doppelzimmer mit Bad?
hab-en zee yn dop-el-tsim-er mit bat

Do you have a room with twin beds and a shower?
Haben Sie ein Zweibettzimmer mit Dusche?
hab-en zee yn svy-bet-tsim-er mit doosh-e

Do you have a single room?
Haben Sie ein Einzelzimmer?
hab-en zee yn yn-tsel-tsim-er

Reservations and enquiries

I need a double room with a bed for a child
Ich brauche ein Doppelzimmer mit Kinderbett
*eekh **browkh**-e yn **dop**-el-tsim-er mit **kind**-er-bet*

I need — a single room with a shower or bath
Ich brauche — ein Einzelzimmer mit Dusche oder Bad
*eekh **browkh**-e — yn **yn**-tsel-tsim-er mit **doosh**-e oad-er **bat***

— a room with a double bed
— ein Doppelzimmer
*— yn **dop**-el-tsim-er*

— a room with twin beds and bath
— ein Zweibettzimmer mit Bad
*— yn **tsvy**-bet-tsim-er mit **bat***

— a single room
— ein Einzelzimmer
*— yn **yn**-tsel-stim-er*

How much is — full board?
Wieviel kostet — Vollpension?
*vee-**feel kost**-et — **fol**-pen-see-**oan***

— half-board?
— Halbpension?
*— **halp**-pen-see-**oan***

— it per night?
— es pro Nacht?
*— es pro **nakht***

38

Reservations and enquiries

       — the room per night?
       — das Zimmer pro Nacht?
       *— das **tsim**-er pro **nakht***

Do you take traveller's cheques?
Nehmen Sie Reiseschecks?
***naym**-en zee **ryz**-e-sheks*

Does the price include — room and breakfast?
    Beinhaltet der Preis — Übernachtung und Frühstück
    *be-**in**-halt-et der **prys** —**ûb**-er-nakht-oong oont **frû**shtook*

                 — room and all meals?
                 — Übernachtung und alle
                    Mahlzeiten
                 *— **ûb**-er-nakht-oong oont al-e*
                   * **mal**-tsyt-en*

                 — room and dinner?
                 — Übernachtung und Abendessen
                 *— **ûb**-ernakht-oong ont **ab**-ent-es-en*

Can we have adjoining rooms?
Könnten wir Zimmer nebeneinander haben?
***koent**-en veer **tsim**-er nay-ben-yn-**and**-er **hab**-en*

Do you have a car park?
Haben Sie einen Gästeparkplatz?
***hab**-en zee yn-en **gest**-e-park-plats*

Reservations and enquiries

Do you have a cot for my baby?
Haben Sie ein Kinderbett für mein Baby?
hab-en zee yn kind-er-bet fûr myn bayb-ee

Are there supervised activities for the children?
Gibt es beaufsichtigte Aktivitäten für Kinder?
gipt es be-owf-zeekht-eegt-e ak-teev-ee-tet-en fûr kind-er

Can my son sleep in our room?
Kann mein Sohn in unserem Zimmer schlafen?
kan myn zoan in oonz-er-em tsim-er shlaf-en

Are there other children staying at the hotel?
Wohnen noch andere Kinder in diesem Hotel?
voan-en nokh and-er-e kind-er in deez-em hoa-tel

Do you have a fax machine?
Haben Sie ein Faxgerät?
hab-en zee yn fax-ge-ret

Do you have a laundry service?
Haben Sie einen Waschdienst?
hab-en zee yn-en vash-deenst

Do you have a safe for valuables?
Haben Sie einen Safe für Wertsachen?
hab-en zee yn-en sayf fûr vert-zakh-en

Do you have any English newspapers?
Haben Sie englische Zeitungen?
hab-en zee eng-leesh-e tsyt-oong-en

Reservations and enquiries

Do you have satellite TV?
Haben Sie Satellitenfernsehen?
hab-en zee za-te-leet-en-fern-zay-en

Which floor is my room on?
Auf welchem Stock ist mein Zimmer?
owf velkh-em shtok ist myn tsim-er

Is there a casino?
Gibt es hier ein Kasino?
gipt es heer yn ka-see-noa

Is there a hairdryer?
Gibt es einen Föhn?
gipt es yn-en foen

Is there a lift?
Haben Sie einen Aufzug?
hab-en zee yn-en owf-tsoog

Is there a minibar?
Gibt es eine Minibar?
gipt es yn-e meen-ee-bar

Is there a sauna?
Haben Sie eine Sauna?
hab-en zee yn-e zown-a

Is there a swimming pool?
Haben Sie ein Schwimmbecken?
hab-en zee yn shvim-bek-en

41

Reservations and enquiries

Is there a telephone?
Gibt es ein Telefon?
gipt es yn tay-lay-foan

Is there a television?
Gibt es ein Fernsehgerät?
gipt es yn fern-zay-ge-ret

Is there a trouser press?
Gibt es eine Hosenpresse?
gipt es yn-e hoaz-en-pres-e

What is the voltage here?
Wie hoch ist die Spannung hier?
vee hoakh ist dee shpan-oong heer

Is the voltage 220 or 110?
Beträgt die Spannung 220 oder 110 Volt?
*be-tregt dee shpan-oong tsvy-hoond-ert-tsvan-tseekh oad-
er hoond-ert-tsayn volt*

Is this a safe area?
Ist das eine sichere Gegend?
ist das yn-e zeekh-er-e gay-gent

Is there a market in the town?
Gibt es in dieser Stadt einen Markt?
gipt es in deez-er shtat yn-en markt

Reservations and enquiries

Can you recommend a good local restaurant?
Können Sie ein gutes Restaurant in der Nähe empfehlen?
*koen-en zee yn **goot**-es rest-oa-**rong** in der **ne**-e emp-**fayl**-en*

Is there a Chinese restaurant?
Gibt es hier ein chinesisches Lokal?
gipt** es **heer** yn khee-**nayz**-eesh-es loa-**kal

Is there an Indian restaurant?
Gibt es hier ein indisches Lokal?
gipt** es **heer** yn **in**-deesh-es loa-**kal

Can I use traveller's cheques?
Kann ich mit Reiseschecks zahlen?
***kan** eekh mit **ryz**-e-sheks **tsal**-en*

Has my colleague arrived yet?
Ist mein Kollege schon angekommen?
*ist myn ko-**layg**-e shoan **an**-ge-kom-en*

What time does the restaurant close?
Wann schließt das Restaurant?
*van **shleest** das rest-oa-**rong***

When does the bar open?
Wann öffnet die Bar?
*van **oef**-net dee **bar***

What time does the hotel close?
Wann schließt das Hotel?
*van **shleest** das hoa-**tel***

Service

What time is — breakfast?
Wann wird das — Frühstück — serviert?
van virt das — frû-shtûk — zer-veert

> **— dinner?**
> — das Abendessen?
> — *das a-bent-es-en*

> **— lunch?**
> — das Mittagessen?
> — *das mi-tag-es-en*

Service

Can I make a telephone call from here?
Kann ich von hier aus telefonieren?
kan eekh fon heer ows tay-lay-fo-neer-en

Can I dial direct from my room?
Kann ich von meinem Zimmer aus direkt wählen?
kan eekh fon myn-em tsim-er ows dee-rekt vel-en

Can I have an outside line?
Könnte ich eine Verbindung nach draußen haben?
koent-e eekh yn-e fer-bind-oong nakh drows-en hab-en

Can I charge this to my room?
Kann ich das auf meine Rechnung setzen lassen?
kan eekh das owf myn-e rekh-noong zets-en las-en

Can I have my key, please?
Kann ich bitte meinen Schlüssel haben?
kan eekh bit-e myn-en shlûs-el hab-en

Can I have — a newspaper?
Kann ich — eine Zeitung haben?
kan eekh — yn-e tsyt-oong hab-en

— **an ashtray?**
— einen Aschenbecher?
— *yn-en ash-en-bekh-er*

— **another blanket?**
— noch eine Decke?
— *nokh yn-e dek-e*

— **another pillow?**
— noch ein Kissen?
— *nokh yn kis-en*

Can I have my wallet from the safe?
Könnten Sie mir bitte meine Brieftasche aus dem Safe
geben?
*koent-en zee meer bit-e myn-e breef-tash-e ows dem sayf
gayb-en*

Can I hire a portable telephone?
Kann ich ein tragbares Telefon mieten?
kan eekh yn trag-bar-es tay-lay-foan meet-en

Service

Can I send this by courier?
Kann ich das per Kurier schicken?
*kan eekh das per koo-**reer** shik-en*

Can I use my charge card?
Kann ich meine Kundenkreditkarte verwenden?
*kan eekh myn-e **koond**-en kray-**deet**-kart-e fer-**vend**-en*

Can I use my personal computer here?
Kann ich meinen Computer hier verwenden?
*kan eekh myn-en com-**pyoot**-er heer fer-**vend**-en*

Can we have breakfast in our room, please?
Können wir bitte in unserem Zimmer frühstücken?
*koen-en veer **bit**-e in oons-er-em tsim-er frû-shtûk-en*

Is there a room service menu?
Gibt es eine Karte für den Zimmerservice?
*gipt es yn-e **kart**-e fûr den tsim-er-zer-**vees***

I need an early morning call
Ich möchte morgen früh geweckt werden
*eekh **moekht**-e mor-gen frû ge-**vekt** vayrd-en*

Is there a trouser press I can use?
Gibt es eine Hosenpresse, die ich verwenden kann?
*gipt es yn-e **hoaz**-en-pres-e dee eekh fer-**vend**-en kan*

I am expecting a fax
Ich erwarte ein Fax
*eekh er-**vart**-e yn **fax***

Where can I send a fax?
Wo kann ich ein Fax senden?
voa kan eekh yn fax send-en

I need to charge these batteries
Ich muß diese Batterien aufladen
eekh moos deez-e bat-er-ee-en owf-lad-en

I want to press these clothes
Ich möchte meine Kleider bügeln
eekh moekht-e myn-e klyd-er bûg-eln

Please can I leave a message?
Kann ich bitte eine Nachricht hinterlassen?
kan eekh bit-e yn-e nakh-reekht hint-er-las-en

My room number is 22
Meine Zimmernummer ist 22
myn-e tsim-er-noom-er ist tsvy-oont-tsvan-tseekh

Please fill the minibar
Würden Sie bitte die Minibar wieder auffüllen?
vûrd-en zee bit-e dee meen-ee-bar veed-er owf-fûl-en

I need — a razor
Ich brauche — einen Rasierapparat
eekh browkh-e — yn-en ra-zeer-a-pa-rat

— some soap
— Seife
— zyf-e

Service

— **some toilet paper**
— Toilettenpapier
— *toy-**let**-en-pa-**peer***

— **some towels**
— Handtücher
— ***hant**-tûkh-er*

— **some coat hangers**
— ein paar Bügel
— *yn par **bûg**-el*

— **some writing paper**
— etwas Schreibpapier
— *et-vas **shryb**-pa-**peer***

Please turn the heating off
Würden Sie bitte die Heizung abschalten?
*vûrd-en zee **bit**-e dee **hyts**-oong **ap**-shalt-en*

Please, wake me at 7 o'clock in the morning
Wecken Sie mich bitte um 7 Uhr.
*vek-en zee meekh **bit**-e oom **zeeb**-en oor*

Please send this fax for me
Bitte senden Sie dieses Fax für mich
*bit-e **zend**-en zee **deez**-es **fax** fûr **meekh***

Where is the manager?
Wo ist der Manager?
*voa ist der **man**-a-ger*

Can I speak to the manager?
Kann ich mit dem Manager sprechen?
*kan eekh mit dem **man**-a-ger **shprekh**-en*

Hello, this is the manager
Guten Tag, hier spricht der Direktor
***goot**-en **tag** heer sprikht der di-**rek**-tor*

Problems

I cannot close the window
Ich kann das Fenster nicht schließen
*eekh kan das **fenst**-er neekht **shlees**-en*

I cannot open the window
Ich kann das Fenster nicht öffnen
*eekh kan das **fenst**-er neekht **oef**-nen*

The air conditioning is not working
Die Klimaanlage funktioniert nicht
*dee **kleem**-a-an-lag-e foonk-tsee-o-**neert** neekht*

The bathroom is dirty
Das Badezimmer ist schmutzig
*das **bad**-e-tsim-er ist **shmootz**-eekh*

The heating is not working
Die Heizung funktioniert nicht
*dee **hyts**-oong foonk-tsee-o-**neert** neekht*

Problems

The light is not working
Das Licht funktioniert nicht
*das **leekht** foonk-tsee-o-**neert** neekht*

The room is not serviced
Für dieses Zimmer besteht kein Zimmerservice
*fûr dees-es **tsim**-er be-shtayt kyn **tsim**-er-ser-vees*

The room is too noisy
Das Zimmer ist zu laut
*das **tsim**-er ist tsoo **lowt***

The room key does not work
Der Zimmerschlüssel funktioniert nicht
*der **tsim**-er-shlûs-el foonk-tsee-o-**neert** neekht*

There are no towels in the room
In dem Zimmer sind keine Handtücher
*in dem **tsim**-er zint kyn-e **hant**-tûkh-er*

There is no hot water
Wir haben kein heißes Wasser
*veer **hab**-en kyn **hys**-es **vas**-er*

There is no plug for the washbasin
Im Waschbecken ist kein Stöpsel
*im **vash**-bek-en ist kyn **shtoep**-sel*

Checking out

We will be leaving early tomorrow
Wir werden morgen früh abfahren
*veer vayrd-en **morg**-en frû **ap**-far-en*

I have to leave tomorrow
Ich muß morgen wegfahren
*eekh **moos morg**-en **vayg**-far-en*

Can I have the bill please?
Kann ich bitte die Rechnung haben?
***kan** eekh bit-e dee **rekh**-noong hab-en*

I want to stay an extra night
Ich möchte eine Nacht länger bleiben
*eekh **moekht**-e yn-e **nakht leng**-er **blyb**-en*

Do I have to change rooms?
Muß ich in ein anderes Zimmer ziehen?
*moos eekh in yn **and**-er-es **tsim**-er **tsee**-en*

Could you have my bags brought down?
Könnten Sie mein Gepäck bitte herunterbringen lassen?
***koent**-en zee myn ge-**pek** bit-e hayr-**oont**-er-**bring**-en **las**-en*

Please leave the bags in the lobby
Lassen Sie das Gepäck bitte in der Eingangshalle stehen
***las**-en zee das ge-**pek** bit-e in der **yn**-gangs-hal-e **shtay**-en*

Checking out

Could you order me a taxi?
Könnten Sie bitte ein Taxi rufen?
*koent-en zee **bit**-e yn **tax**-ee **roof**-en*

Thank you, we enjoyed our stay
Vielen Dank, wir hatten einen sehr angenehmen Aufenthalt
*feel-en **dank** veer hat-en yn-en **zayk** an-gen-naym-en
owf-ent-halt*

OTHER ACCOMMODATION

Apartment and villa rental

A furnished rental with cooking facilities can save money, but they are often luxury properties, economical only if your party is large. The German Automobile Association issues listings of family holiday apartments or contact local tourist offices.

Renting a house

We have rented this villa
Wir haben dieses Ferienhaus gemietet
*veer **hab**-en deez-es **fayr**-i-en-hows ge-**meet**-et*

Here is our booking form
Hier ist unser Buchungsformular
heer** ist unz-er **bookh**-oongs-form-oo-**lar

We need two sets of keys
Wir brauchen die Schlüssel in zweifacher Ausführung
*veer **browkh**-en dee **shlûs**-el in **tsvy**-fakh-er **ows**-fûr-oong*

Renting a house

When does the cleaner come?
Wann kommt die Putzfrau?
*van komt dee **poots**-frow*

Where is the bathroom?
Wo ist das Badezimmer?
*voa ist das **bad**-e-tsim-er*

Can I contact you on this number?
Kann ich Sie unter dieser Nummer erreichen?
*kan eekh zee oont-er deez-er **noom**-er er-**rykh**-en*

Can you send a repairman?
Können Sie jemanden zum Reparieren schicken?
*koen-en zee **jaym**-an-den tsoom re-pa-**reer**-en **shik**-en*

How does this work?
Wie funktioniert das?
*vee foonk-tsee-o-**neert** das*

I cannot open the shutters
Ich kann die Fensterläden nicht öffnen
*eekh kan dee **fenst**-er-**led**-en neekht **oef**-nen*

Is the water heater working?
Funktioniert der Warmwasserbereiter
*foonk-tsee-o-**neert** der **varm**-vas-er-be-**ry**-ter*

Is the water safe to drink?
Kann man das Wasser unbedenklich trinken?
*kan man das **vas**-er **oon**-be-denk-leekh **trink**-en*

Renting a house

Is there any spare bedding?
Gibt es zusätzliches Bettzeug?
gipt es tsoo-zets-leekh-es bet-tsoyg

The cooker does not work
Der Herd funktioniert nicht
der hert foonk-tsee-o-neert neekht

The refrigerator does not work
Der Kühlschrank funktioniert nicht
der kûl-shrank foonk-tsee-o-neert neekht

The toilet is blocked
Die Toilette ist verstopft
dee toy-let-e ist fer-shtopft

There is a leak
Da ist eine undichte Stelle
da ist yn-e oon-deekht-e shtel-e

We do not have any water
Wir haben kein Wasser
veer hab-en kyn vas-er

Where is the fuse box?
Wo ist der Sicherungskasten?
voa ist der zeekh-er-oongs-kast-en

Where is the key for this door?
Wo ist der Schlüssel für diese Tür?
voa ist der shlûs-el fûr deez-e tur

Around the house

Where is the socket for my razor?
Wo ist die Steckdose für meinen Rasierapparat?
*voa ist dee **shtek**-doz-e fûr myn-en ra-**zeer**-ap-a-**rat***

Around the house

bath
Bad
bat

bathroom
Badezimmer
***bad**-e-tsim-er*

bed
Bett
bet

brush
Bürste
***bûrst**-e*

can opener
Dosenöffner
***doaz**-en-oef-ner*

chair
Stuhl
shtool

cooker
Herd
hert

corkscrew
Korkenzieher
***kork**-en-tsee-er*

cup
Tasse
***tas**-e*

fork
Gabel
***gab**-el*

glass
Glas
glas

kitchen
Küche
***kûkh**-e*

56

knife
Messer
mes-er

spoon
Löffel
loef-el

mirror
Spiegel
shpeeg-el

stove
Ofen
oa-fen

pan
Pfanne
pfan-e

table
Tisch
tish

plate
Teller
tel-er

tap
Wasserhahn
was-er-han

refrigerator
Kühlschrank
kûl-shrank

toilet
Toilette
toy-let-e

sheet
Bettuch
bet-tookh

vacuum cleaner
Staubsauger
shtowp-zowg-er

sink
Spüle
shpû-le

washbasin
Waschbecken
vash-bek-en

Camping

There are some 2000 camp sites scattered all over Germany, 400 of which are open in the winter. If you enjoy a down-to-earth holiday, this is for you. Some sites will lend you a tent for a small fee. Blue signs with a black tent on a white background indicate official sites. The German Camping Club (DCC, Mandlstrasse 28, D-80802 Munich) publishes a list of sites, including details about trailer and caravan facilities.

If you want to camp rough, you need the permission of the landowner. The police will help you to contact him or her.

Caravans may be parked by the roadside for one night only but you may not set up equipment there.

Camping questions

Can we camp in your field?
Können wir auf Ihrem Feld zelten?
*koen-en veer owf **eer-em felt** tselt-en*

Can we camp near here?
Können wir hier in der Nähe zelten?
*koen-en veer heer in der **ne-e tselt**-en*

Can we park our caravan here?
Können wir unseren Caravan hier parken?
*koen-en veer oons-er-en **ka**-ra-van heer **park**-en*

Do I pay in advance?
Zahle ich im voraus?
tsal-e eekh im foar-ows

Do I pay when I leave?
Zahle ich bei der Abreise?
tsal-e eekh by der ap-ryz-e

Is there a more sheltered site?
Gibt es einen geschützteren Platz?
gipt es yn-en ge-shûts-ter-en plats

Is there a restaurant or a shop on the site?
Gibt es auf dem Platz ein Restaurant oder einen Laden?
gipt es owf dem plats yn rest-o-rong od-er yn-en lad-en

Is there another camp site near there?
Gibt es einen anderen Campingplatz in der Nähe?
gipt es yn-en and-er-en kamp-ing-plats in der ne-e

Is this the drinking water?
Ist das Trinkwasser?
ist das trink-vas-er

Please can we pitch our tent here?
Können wir bitte unser Zelt hier aufstellen?
koen-en veer bit-e oons-er tselt heer owf-shtel-en

The site is very wet and muddy
Das Gelände ist sehr naß und schlammig
das ge-lend-e ist zayr nas oont shlam-eekh

Around the camp site

Where are the toilets?
Wo sind die Toiletten?
voa zint dee toy-let-en

Where can I have a shower?
Wo kann ich mich duschen?
voa kan eekh meekh doosh-en

Where can we wash our dishes?
Wo kann ich unser Geschirr abspülen?
voa kan eekh oons-er ge-shir ap-shpül-en

Around the camp site

air mattress
Luftmatratze
looft-ma-trats-e

bottle-opener
Flaschenöffner
flash-en-oef-ner

bucket
Eimer
ym-er

camp bed
Feldbett
felt-bet

camp chair
Klappstuhl
klap-shtool

can-opener
Dosenöffner
doz-en-oef-ner

candle
Kerze
kerts-e

cup
Tasse
tas-e

fire
Feuer
foy-er

fly sheet
Fliegennetz
fleeg-en-nets

fork
Gabel
gab-el

frying pan
Bratpfanne
brat-pfan-e

ground sheet
Bodenabdeckung
boad-en-ap-dek-oong

guy line
Zeltleine
tselt-lyn-e

knife
Messer
mes-er

mallet
Holzhammer
holts-ham-er

matches
Streichhölzer
shtrykh-hoelts-er

penknife
Taschenmesser
tash-en-mes-er

plate
Teller
tel-er

rucksack
Rucksack
rook-zak

sleeping bag
Schlafsack
shlaf-zak

spoon
Löffel
loef-el

stove
Ofen
oaf-en

tent peg
Hering
hayr-ing

Hostelling

tent pole
Zeltstange
tselt-shtang-e

thermos flask
Thermosflasche
ter-moas-flash-e

tent
Zelt
tselt

torch
Taschenlampe
tash-en-lamp-e

Hostelling

German youth hostels (*Jugendherberge*) have long lost their army camp atmosphere and are probably the most efficient and up-to-date in the world. There are more than 600, and many of the originally low budget dormitories have been turned into new leisure centres, which also offer courses. A new development is that of offering insights into ecological issues with excursions and open-air studies. Many eastern youth hostels had to close down following reunification, but efforts are currently being made to bring them up to western standards. Apart from Bavaria, where there is an age limit of 27, there are no restrictions of age, although those under 20 get preference. For information, write to Deutsches Jugendherbergswerk, Bismarckstrasse 8, Postfach 1455, 32756 Detmold.

Are you open during the day?
Sind Sie tagsüber geöffnet?
zint zee tags-üb-er ge-oef-net

Can I join here?
Können wir hier Mitglied werden?
koen-en veer heer mit-gleet vayrd-en

Can I use the kitchen?
Kann ich die Küche benutzen?
kan eekh dee kûkh-e be-noots-en

Can we stay five nights here?
Können wir fünf Nächte hier bleiben?
koen-en veer fûnf nekht-e heer blyb-en

Can we stay until Sunday?
Können wir bis Sonntag bleiben?
koen-en veer bis zon-tag blyb-en

Do you serve meals?
Servieren Sie auch Mahlzeiten?
ser-veer-en zee owkh mal-tsyt-en

— to take away?
— zum Mitnehmen?
— tsoom mit-naym-en

Here is my membership card
Hier ist meine Mitgliedschaftskarte
heer ist myn-e mit-gleet-shafts-kart-e

I do not have my card
Ich habe meine Karte nicht
eekh hab-e myn-e kart-e neekht

Childcare

Is there a youth hostel near here?
Gibt es eine Jugendherberge in der Nähe?
gipt es yn-e yoog-ent-hayr-berg-e in der ne-e

What time do you close?
Wann schließen Sie?
van shlees-en zee

Childcare

There is plenty of entertainment available for young travellers. Most cities have children's theatres, numerous playgrounds, theme parks, children's movies at the cinemas during the daytime, and the country's puppet theatres rank among the best in the world. If you are renting a car, be sure to arrange for a child seat. For recommended baby sitters check with your hotel desk. Updated lists are also available from the local tourist office.

Can you warm this milk for me?
Können Sie mir diese Milch aufwärmen?
koen-en zee meer deez-e milkh owf-verm-en

Do you have a high chair?
Haben Sie einen Hochstuhl?
hab-en zee yn-en hoakh-shtool

How old is your daughter?
Wie alt ist Ihre Tochter?
vee alt ist eer-e tokht-er

I am very sorry. That was very naughty of him
Tut mir sehr leid. Das war sehr böse von ihm.
toot meer zayr lyt das var zayr boez-e fon eem

Is there a baby-sitter?
Haben Sie einen Babysitter?
hab-en zee yn-en bayb-ee-sit-er

Is there a cot for our baby?
Haben Sie ein Kinderbett für unser Baby?
hab-en zee yn kind-er-bet fûr oons-er bayb-ee

Is there a paddling pool?
Haben Sie ein Planschbecken?
hab-en zee yn plansh-bek-en

Is there a swimming pool?
Haben Sie ein Schwimmbecken?
hab-en zee yn shvim-bek-en

Is there a swing park?
Haben Sie Schaukeln?
hab-en zee showk-eln

It will not happen again
Es wird nicht wieder vorkommen
es virt neekht veed-er foar-kom-en

My daughter is 7 years old
Meine Tochter ist sieben Jahre alt
myn-e tokht-er ist zeeb-en yar-e alt

Childcare

My son is 10 years old
Mein Sohn ist zehn Jahre alt
myn zoan ist tsayn yar-e alt

She goes to bed at nine o'clock
Sie geht um neun Uhr ins Bett
zee gayt oom noyn oor ins bet

We will be back in two hours
Wir sind in zwei Stunden zurück
veer zind in tsvy shtoond-en tsoo-rûk

Where can I buy some disposable nappies?
Wo kann ich Wegwerfwindeln kaufen?
voa kan eekh veg-verf-vin-deln kowf-en

Where can I change the baby?
Wo kann ich das Baby wickeln?
voa kan eekh das bayb-ee vik-eln

Where can I feed/breastfeed my baby?
Wo kann ich mein Baby füttern/stillen?
voa kan eekh myn bayb-ee fût-ern/shtil-en

GETTING AROUND

Tourist offices

Most German towns are served by a local tourist office, which is usually located in the town square or the main train station. These offices can have a variety of bewildering names – *Verkehrsamt, Fremdenverkehrsbüro, Fremdenverkehrsverein, Tourist-Information, Gemeindeamt,* and in spa-towns *Kurverwaltung* or *Kurverein.*

Business hours

Bank opening times vary from state to state, but they are generally open on weekdays from 8.30am or 9am to 2pm or 3pm (5pm or 6pm on Thursday) with a lunchbreak of about an hour. Most museums are open from Tuesday to Sunday 9am–6pm, many stay open late on Wednesday and Thursday. Post offices in larger cities are usually open from 8am to 6pm Monday to Friday and on Saturday until noon. Department stores are generally open from 9am or 9.15am to 8pm on weekdays and until 2pm on Saturdays. Many shops, however, still stick to the business hours in operation before liberalisation in 1996 and close at 6pm or 6.30pm. In 1997 some department stores were thinking of following suit.

Asking for directions

Where is — the art gallery?
  Wo ist — die Kunstgalerie?
  voa ist — dee koonst-gal-er-ee

  — the post office?
  — das Postamt?
  — *das post-amt*

  — the Tourist Information Service?
  — die Tourist Information?
  — *dee too-reest in-form-a-tsee-oan*

Can you show me on the map?
Können Sie mir das auf der Karte zeigen?
koen-en zee meer das owf der kart-e tsyg-en

Can you tell me the way to the station?
Können Sie mir den Weg zum Bahnhof sagen?
koen-en zee meer den vayg tsoom ban-hoaf zag-en

Can you walk there?
Kann man dorthin zu Fuß gehen?
kan man dort-hin tsoo foos gay-en

I am looking for the Tourist Information Office
Ich suche die Tourist Information
eekh zookh-e dee too-reest in-form-a-tsee-oan

Where are the toilets?
Wo sind die Toiletten?
voa zint dee toy-let-en

I am lost
Ich habe mich verlaufen
eekh hab-e meekh fer-lowf-en

I am lost. How do I get to the Krone Hotel?
Ich habe mich verlaufen. Wie finde ich das Hotel Krone?
eekh hab-e meekh fer-lowf-en vee find-e eekh das hoa-tel kroan-e

I am trying to get to the market
Ich versuche, zum Markt zu gehen
eekh fer-zookh-e tsoom markt tsoo gay-en

I want to go to the theatre
Ich möchte ins Theater gehen
eekh moekht-e ins tay-a-ter gay-en

Is it far?
Ist es weit?
ist es vyt

Is there a bus that goes there?
Gibt es einen Bus, der dorthin fährt?
gipt es yn-en boos der dort-hin fert

Is there a train that goes there?
Gibt es einen Zug, der dorthin fährt?
gipt es yn-en tsoog der dort-hin fert

69

Directions — by road

Is this the right way to the supermarket?
Ist das der richtige Weg zum Supermarkt?
*ist **das** der **reekht**-ig-e **vayg** tsoom **soop**-er-markt*

We are looking for a restaurant
Wir suchen ein Restaurant
*veer **zookh**-en yn rest-oa-**rong***

Where do I get a bus for the city centre?
Wo finde ich einen Bus zur Innenstadt?
***voa** find-e eekh yn-en **boos** tsoor **in**-en-shtat*

Directions — by road

Do I turn here for Bad Windsheim?
Muß ich nach Bad Windsheim hier abbiegen?
***moos** eekh nakh bat **vints**-hym heer **ap**-beeg-en*

How far is it to Dresden?
Wie weit ist es nach Dresden?
*vee **vyt** ist es nakh **drays**-den*

How long will it take to get there?
Wie lange dauert es, bis man dorthin kommt?
*vee **lang**-e dow-ert es bis man **dort**-hin komt*

Is there a filling station near here?
Gibt es hier in der Nähe eine Tankstelle?
***gipt** es heer in der **ne**-e yn-e **tank**-shtel-e*

Directions — by road

I am looking for the next exit
Ich suche die nächste Ausfahrt
eekh zookh-e dee nekst-e ows-fart

Where does this road go to?
Wohin führt diese Straße?
voa-heen fûrt deez-e shtras-e

How do I get onto the motorway?
Wie komme ich auf die Autobahn?
vee kom-e eekh owf dee owt-o-ban

Which is the best route to Frankfurt?
Wie komme ich am besten nach Frankfurt?
vee kom-e eekh am best-en nakh frank-foort

Which road do I take to Aachen?
Welche Straße muß ich nach Aachen nehmen?
velkh-e shtras-e moos eekh nakh akh-en naym-en

Which is the fastest route?
Was ist die schnellste Route?
vas ist dee shnelst-e root-e

Will we arrive in time for dinner?
Werden wir rechtzeitig zum Abendessen ankommen?
vayrd-en veer rekht-tsyt-eekh tsoom ab-end-es-en an-kom-en

71

Directions — what you may hear

Sie fahren — bis...
zee far-en — bis...
　You go — as far as...

　　　　— nach links
　　　　— nakh links
　　　　— left

　　　　— nach rechts
　　　　— nakh rekhts
　　　　— right

　　　　— auf . . . zu
　　　　— owf . . . tsoo
　　　　— towards . . .

Es ist — an der Kreuzung
es ist — an der kroyts-oong
　It is — at the crossroads

　　　　— unter der Brücke
　　　　— oont-er der brûk-e
　　　　— under the bridge

　　　　— nach der Ampel
　　　　— nakh der amp-el
　　　　— after the traffic lights

Directions — what you may hear

— um die Ecke
— oom dee ek-e
— around the corner

— neben dem Kino
— nayb-en dem keen-o
— next to the cinema

— auf dem nächsten Stockwerk
— owf dem nekst-en shtok-verk
— on the next floor

— gegenüber dem Bahnhof
— gayg-en-ûb-er dem ban-hoaf
— opposite the railway station

— da drüben
— da drûb-en
— over there

Überqueren Sie die Straße
ûb-er-kvayr-en zee dee shtras-e
Cross the street

Biegen Sie links ab
beeg-en zee links ap
Turn left

Biegen Sie rechts ab
beeg-en zee rekhts ap
Turn right

Directions — what you may hear

Folgen Sie den Zeichen nach . . .
folg-en zee den tsykh-en nakh . . .
Follow the signs for . . .

— die Autobahn
— dee owt-o-ban
— the motorway

— die nächste Abzweigung
— dee nekst-e ap-tsvyg-oong
— the next junction

— der Platz
— der plats
— the square

Fahren Sie gerade aus
far-en zee ge-rad-e ows
Keep going straight ahead

Biegen Sie bei der nächsten Straße rechts ab
beeg-en zee by der nekst-en shtras-e rekhts ap
Take the first road on the right

Sie müssen zurückfahren
zee mûs-en tsoo-rûk-far-en
You have to go back

Nehmen Sie die Straße nach Bamberg
naym-en zee dee stras-e nakh bam-berg
Take the road for Bamberg

74

Biegen Sie bei der zweiten Straße links ab
beeg-en zee by der tsvyt-en stras-e links ap
Take the second road on the left

Sie müssen eine Gebühr zahlen
zee mûs-en yn-e ge-bûr tsal-en
You have to pay the toll

Hiring a car

Major car hire agencies are: Budget, Eurodollar, Hertz and Europcar Inter-Rent. To get the best deal, book through a travel agent who is prepared to shop around and look into wholesalers (Auto Europe, Europe by Car, DER Tours, the Kemwel Group).

You are generally responsible for any damage or loss of the vehicle. It is best to check what coverage you have under your own personal insurance as well as credit card insurance. Stolen vehicles are often not covered by insurance sold by car-rental companies. Ask about drop-off charges, if you plan to pick up your car in one city and leave it in another.

You will not need your driving licence translated if you are from Andorra, Belgium, Cyprus, Denmark, Finland, France, Great Britain, Greece, Hong Kong, Hungary, Ireland, Italy, Luxembourg, Monaco, the Netherlands, New Zealand, Norway, Portugal, San Marino, Sweden, Switzerland, Senegal or Spain.

Hiring a car

Can I hire a car?
Kann ich einen Wagen mieten?
*kan eekh yn-en **vag**-en **meet**-en*

Can I hire a car with an automatic gearbox?
Kann ich einen Wagen mit Automatikschaltung mieten?
*kan eekh yn-en **vag**-en mit owt-o-**mat**-eek-**shalt**-oong **meet**-en*

I want to hire a car
Ich möchte einen Wagen mieten
*eekh **moekht**-e yn-en **vag**-en **meet**-en*

I need it for 2 weeks
Ich brauche ihn für zwei Wochen
*eekh **browkh**-e een fûr tsvy **vokh**-en*

We will both be driving
Wir werden beide fahren
*veer **vayrd**-en **byd**-e far-en*

Do you have — a large car?
Haben Sie — einen großen Wagen?
*hab-en zee — yn-en **gros**-en **vag**-en*

— a smaller car?
— einen kleineren Wagen?
*— eyn-en **klyn**-er-en **vag**-en*

— an automatic?
— einen Wagen mit Automatikschaltung?
*— yn-en **vag**-en mit owt-oa-**mat**-ik-**shalt**-oong*

— **an estate car?**
— einen Kombiwagen?
— *yn-en kom-bee-vag-en*

I would like to leave the car at the airport
Ich möchte den Wagen am Flughafen stehen lassen
eekh moekht-e den vag-en am floog-haf-en shtay-en las-en

I want to leave the car at the airport
Ich möchte den Wagen am Flughafen lassen
eekh moekht-e den vag-en am floog-haf-en las-en

Is there a charge per kilometre?
Gibt es eine Gebühr pro Kilometer?
gipt es yn-e ge-bûr pro keel-o-mayt-er

Must I return the car here?
Muß ich den Wagen hierher zurückbringen?
moos eekh den vag-en heer-hayr tsu-rûk-bring-en

Please explain the documents
Bitte erklären Sie mir die Unterlagen
bit-e er-kler-en zee meer dee oont-er-lag-en

How much is it per kilometre?
Wieviel kostet es pro Kilometer?
vee-feel kost-et es pro keel-o-mayt-er

Can I pay for insurance?
Kann ich gegen Gebühr eine Versicherung abschließen?
kan eekh gayg-en ge-bûr yn-e fer-zeekh-er-oong ap-shlees-en

Hiring a car

Do I have to pay a deposit?
Muß ich etwas anzahlen?
*moos eekh et-vas **an**-tsal-en*

I would like a spare set of keys
Ich hätte gerne Extraschlüssel
*eekh **het**-e gern-e **ex**-tra-shlûs-el*

How does the steering lock work?
Wie funktioniert das Lenkradschloß?
*vee foonk-tsee-o-**neert** das **lenk**-rat-shlos*

    Please show me how — to operate the lights
Zeigen Sie mir bitte, wie — die Scheinwerfer bedient
                    werden
*tsyg-en zee meer **bit**-e vee — dee **shyn**-verf-er be-**deent**
                    vayrd-en*

    — to operate the windscreen wipers
    — die Scheibenwischer betätigt
        werden
    *— dee **shyb**-en-vish-er be-**tet**-eegt vayrd-en*

Where is reverse gear?
Wo ist der Rückwärtsgang?
*voa ist der **rûk**-verts-gang*

Where is the tool kit?
Wo ist das Werkzeug?
*voa ist das **verk**-tsoyg*

By taxi

German taxis are easily distinguished by the 'taxi' sign on the top. They are usually cream coloured, comfortable saloon cars, which can be hailed at stations, taxi ranks or in the street, and rates are metered. There are also some private hire firms with cars displaying phone numbers. In general try to use the efficient public transport services available in the cities in preference to taxis, which are very expensive.

Please show us around the town
Zeigen Sie uns bitte die Stadt
*tsyg-en zee oons **bit**-e dee **shtat***

Please take me to this address
Bringen Sie mich bitte zu dieser Adresse
***bring**-en zee meekh **bit**-e tsoo **deez**-er a-**dress**-e*

Take me to the airport, please
Bringen Sie mich bitte zum Flughafen
***bring**-en zee meekh **bit**-e tsoom **floog**-haf-en*

The bus station, please
Die Bushaltestelle, bitte
*dee **boos**-halt-e-shtel-e **bit**-e*

By taxi

Turn left, please
Nach links, bitte
*nakh **links** bit-e*

Turn right, please
Nach rechts, bitte
*nakh **rekhts** bit-e*

Can you come back in one hour?
Können Sie in einer Stunde zurückkommen?
***koen**-en zee in **yn**-er **shtoond**-e tsoo-**rûk**-kom-en*

Will you put the bags in the boot?
Könnten Sie das Gepäck bitte in den Kofferraum legen?
***koent**-en zee das ge-**pek** bit-e in den **kof**-er-rowm **layg**-en*

I am in a hurry
Ich bin in Eile
*eekh bin in **yl**-e*

Please hurry, I am late
Bitte beeilen Sie sich, ich habe bereits Verspätung
*bit-e be-**yl**-en zee zeekh eekh **hab**-e be-**ryts** fer-**shpet**-oong*

Please wait here for a few minutes
Bitte warten Sie hier ein paar Minuten
*bit-e **vart**-en zee **heer** yn par mee-**noot**-en*

Please, stop at the corner
An der Ecke bitte halten
*an der **ek**-e bit-e **halt**-en*

Please, wait here
Bitte warten Sie hier
*bit-e **vart**-en zee **heer***

Wait for me please
Bitte warten Sie auf mich
*bit-e **vart**-en zee owf **meekh***

How much is that, please?
Was macht das, bitte?
*vas **makht** das **bit**-e*

Keep the change
Der Rest ist für Sie
*der **rest** ist fûr **zee***

By bus

Germany's urban bus services are very efficient, but there is no nationwide network. The railways operate some services (*Bahnbus*), which link with the rail network. For special touring programmes along fascinating tourist routes, write to Deutsche Touring, Am Römerhof 17, D–60426 Frankfurt am Main, or local tourist offices.

All towns operate their own local buses, which often link up with local trams, S-Bahn (local rail links) and U-Bahn (underground). Tickets usually allow you to transfer freely between the various forms of transport. Public transport in cities is invariably fast, clean and efficient.

By bus

Does this bus go to the castle?
Fährt dieser Bus zur Burg?
*fert deez-er **boos** tsoor **boorg***

How frequent is the service?
In welchen Abständen fährt der Bus?
*in **velkh**-em **ap**-stend-en **fert** der **boos***

How long does it take to get to the park?
Wie lange dauert es bis zum Park?
*vee **lang**-e **dow**-ert es bis tsoom **park***

Is there a bus into town?
Gibt es einen Bus in die Stadt?
gipt** es yn-en **boos** in dee **shtat

What is the fare to the city centre?
Was kostet die Fahrt in die Innenstadt?
*vas **kost**-et dee **fart** in dee **in**-en-shtat*

When is the last bus?
Wann geht der letzte Bus?
*van **gayt** der **letst**-e **boos***

Where do I get the bus for the airport?
Wo kann ich den Bus zum Flughafen nehmen?
***voa** kan eekh den **boos** tsoom **floog**-haf-en **naym**-en*

Where should I change?
Wo muß ich umsteigen?
***voa** moos eekh **oom**-shtyg-en*

82

Which bus do I take for the football stadium?
Welcher Bus fährt zum Fußballstadium?
*velkh-er **boos** fert tsoom **foos**-bal-**stad**-ee-oom*

Will you tell me when to get off the bus?
Könnten Sie mir sagen, wann ich aussteigen muß?
koent**-en zee meer **zag**-en van eekh ows-shtyg-en **moos

By train

In 1994 the rail networks of the former East and West Germany were merged under the name of Deutsche Bahn (DB), which is currently being privatised. The renovation of the ancient tracks of the old German Democratic Republic is progressing fast, allowing the extension into there of the high-speed InterCity Express (ICE). InterCity, EuroCity and InterRegio services have also been improved and expanded.

Depending on classification of service, there are varying surcharges on ticket prices, with InterCity Express fares being about 20 per cent more expensive than normal ones. The cheapest and slowest option are the D-class trains.

All overnight InterCity and D-class services have sleepers with a first class service including breakfast. InterCity and InterCity Express trains have restaurant cars or trolley service, while the InterRegio trains have bistro cars.

Major route connections and their timetables are well coordinated and changing trains is easy as usually you need only cross the platform.

By train

You are strongly advised to book your ticket and seat reservation in advance.

There are various rail passes available offering attractive discounts on rail travel. The German Rail Pass allows unlimited travel over a certain period of time and can also be used on KR River Steamers. The EurailPass provides unlimited first-class travel in participating countries as long as the pass is valid, and there is the cheaper and more limited Europass. In addition there are special passes for young people, senior citizens, groups or those combining rail and car travel. Whichever you are considering, you must purchase your pass before arrival, and none of the passes includes seat reservation.

A return (ticket) to Hamburg, please
Eine Rückfahrkarte nach Hamburg, bitte
yn-e rûk-far-kart-e nakh ham-boorg bit-e

A return to Paris, first-class
Eine Rückfahrkarte erster Klasse nach Paris, bitte
yn-e rûk-far-kart-e erst-er klas-e nakh pa-rees bit-e

A single (one-way ticket) to Hanover, please
Eine Einzelfahrkarte (Rückfahrkarte) nach Hannover, bitte
yn-e yn-tsel-far-kart-e (rûk-far-kart-e) nakh han-oaf-er bit-e

Can I buy a return ticket?
Kann ich eine Rückfahrkarte kaufen?
kan eekh yn-e rûk-far-kart-e kowf-en

I want to book a seat on the sleeper to Paris
Ich möchte einen Platz im Schlafwagen nach Paris buchen
*eekh moekht-e yn-en plats im shlaf-vag-en nakh pa-rees
bookh-en*

Second class. A window seat, please
Zweiter Klasse. Einen Fensterplatz, bitte
tsvyt-er klas-e yn-en fenst-er-plats bit-e

What are the times of the trains to Paris?
Was sind die Zeiten für die Züge nach Paris?
vas zint dee tsyt-en fûr dee tsûg-e nakh pa-rees

Where can I buy a ticket?
Wo kann ich eine Fahrkarte kaufen?
voa kan eekh yn-e far-kart-e kowf-en

A smoking compartment, first-class
Ein Raucherabteil erster Klasse
yn rowkh-er-ap-tyl erst-er klas-e

A non-smoking compartment, please
Ein Nichtraucherabteil bitte
yn neekht-rowkh-er-ap-tyl bit-e

When is the next train to Munich?
Wann geht der nächste Zug nach München?
van gayt der nekst-e tsoog nakh mûn-khen

By train

When is the next train to Stuttgart?
Wann geht der nächste Zug nach Stuttgart?
*van gayt der **nekst**-e **tsoog** nakh **shtoot**-gart*

How long do I have before my next train leaves?
Wieviel Zeit habe ich bis zur Abfahrt meines nächsten
  Zuges?
*vee-feel **tsyt** hab-e eekh bis tsoor **ap**-fart myn-es **nekst**-en
  tsoog-es*

Do I have time to go shopping?
Habe ich noch Zeit zum Einkaufen?
***hab**-e eekh nokh **tsyt** tsoom **yn**-kowf-en*

Can I take my bicycle?
Kann ich mein Rad mitnehmen?
***kan** eekh myn **rat** mit-naym-en*

What time does the train leave?
Wann fährt der Zug ab?
***van** fert der **tsoog** ap*

What time is the last train?
Wann geht der letzte Zug?
van** gayt der **letst**-e **tsoog

Where do I have to change?
Wo muß ich umsteigen?
***voa** moos eekh **oom**-shtyg-en*

By train

I want to leave these bags in the left-luggage
Ich möchte diese Taschen bei der Gepäckverwahrung lassen
*eekh **moekht**-e deez-e **tash**-en by der ge-**pek**-fer-**var**-oong **las**-en*

Can I check in my bags?
Kann ich mein Gepäck aufgeben?
***kan** eekh myn ge-**pek** owf-geb-en*

How much is it per bag?
Wieviel kostet es pro Gepäckstück?
*vee-feel **kost**-et es pro ge-**pek**-shtûk*

I shall pick them up this evening
Kann ich sie heute Abend abholen?
***kan** eekh zee hoyt-e **ab**-ent **ap**-hoal-en*

Where do I pick up my bags?
Wo kann ich mein Gepäck abholen?
***voa** kan eekh myn ge-**pek ap**-hoal-en*

Is there — a buffet car / club car?
Gibt es — eine Snackbar / einen Salonwagen?
***gipt** es —yn-e **snak**-bar / yn-en za-**loang**-vag-en*

> **— a dining car?**
> — einen Speisewagen?
> — yn-en **shpyz**-e-vag-en

Is there a restaurant on the train?
Hat der Zug einen Speisewagen?
***hat** der **tsoog** yn-en **shpyz**-e-vag-en*

By train

Where is the departure board (listing)?
Wo ist der Abfahrtsplan?
voa ist der ap-farts-plan

Which platform do I go to?
Zu welchem Bahnsteig muß ich gehen?
tsoo velkh-em ban-shtyg moos eekh gay-en

Is this the platform for Mannheim?
Ist das der richtige Bahnsteig für den Zug nach Mannheim?
ist das der reekht-ig-e ban-shtyg für den tsoog nakh man-hym

Is this a through train?
Ist das ein Direktzug?
ist das yn dee-rekt-tsoog

Is this the Bonn train?
Ist das der Zug nach Bonn?
ist das der tsoog nakh bon

Do we stop at Schwabach?
Halten wir in Schwabach?
halt-en veer in shvab-akh

What time do we get to Hildesheim?
Wann kommen wir in Hildesheim an?
van kom-en veer in hild-es-hym an

Are we at Hof yet?
Sind wir schon in Hof?
zint veer shoan in hoaf

88

Are we on time?
Haben wir Verspätung?
*ha-ben veer fer-**shpe**-toong*

Can you help me with my bags?
Könnten Sie mir bitte mit meinem Gepäck helfen?
***koent**-en zee meer **bit**-e mit myn-em ge-**pek** **helf**-en*

I have lost my ticket
Ich habe meine Fahrkarte verloren
*eekh **hab**-e myn-e **far**-kart-e fer-**loar**-en*

My wife has my ticket
Meine Frau hat meine Fahrkarte
*myn-e **frow** hat myn-e **far**-kart-e*

Is this seat taken?
Ist dieser Platz besetzt?
*ist **deez**-er **plats** be-**zetst***

May I open the window?
Darf ich das Fenster öffnen?
***darf** eekh das **fenst**-er **oef**-nen*

This is a non-smoking compartment
Das ist ein Nichtraucherabteil
das** ist yn **neekht**-rowkh-er-ap-**tyl

This is my seat
Das ist mein Platz
das** ist myn **plats

89

By train

Where is the toilet?
Wo sind die Toiletten?
voa zint dee toy-let-en

Why have we stopped?
Warum haben wir angehalten?
va-room hab-en veer an-ge-halt-en

DRIVING

What you need

Entry formalities are few: you need your domestic licence (*see* Hiring a Car, page 75) and proof of insurance. It is recommended that drivers get a green card from their insurance company, which extends insurance coverage to driving in continental Europe. Extra breakdown insurance and vehicle and personal security coverage are advisable. All foreign cars need a country sticker, and right-hand-drive vehicles should have their headlights adjusted.

Roads

There are many specially designated tourist roads, covering areas of specific scenic or historic interest. The longest one is the *Deutsche Ferienstrasse,* the German Holiday Road, which runs from the Baltic to the Alps, a distance of around 1,720 kilometres (1,070 miles). The most famous, however, is the *Romantische Strasse,* the Romantic Road, which runs from Würzburg in Franconia to Fussen in the Alps, spanning 355 kilometres (220 miles) and passing through some of the most historic cities in Germany.

Roads in the western part of Germany are excellent, with

Rules

10,500 kilometres (6,500 miles) of toll-free motorways (*Autobahnen*) in ultramodern condition. There is no speed limit on motorways except the recommended one of 130 kilometres per hour (62 miles per hour). Germans drive fast, and it is advisable to be very familiar with rules and signs before venturing onto the roads. There are 169 motorway service stations and 268 petrol and diesel stations offering a round-the-clock service. In the east, many road surfaces are still in urgent need of repair and generally the road system is not yet as well developed, especially the main links across the former border, which are insufficient for the increased volume of traffic.

Rules

Driving on the right – it is illegal to pass on the right side of the road, even on motorways. Travellers used to driving on the left should take care on quiet roads, and when taking a left-hand turn should not revert to the left side of the road.

Traffic signs – traffic signs in Germany are international.

Priority to the right – at intersections priority is usually indicated by signs, even when there are traffic lights.

Speed limits – built up areas: 50 kilometres per hour (31 miles per hour); outside built-up areas: 100 kilometres per hour (62 miles per hour). Place-name signs mark the boundaries of built-up areas. The recommended speed limit on motorways: 130 kilometres per hour (62 miles per hour).

Traffic and weather conditions

It is not advisable to drive slowly in the left-hand (fast) lane, as you will soon see cars looming in your rear mirror with headlights flashing. This lane is for overtaking. Cars pulling trailers are limited to 80 kilometres per hour (50 miles per hour).

Seatbelts – seatbelts are required by law, front and back.

Children – children under 12 may not sit in the front seat unless a special seat has been installed; children up to four need a special child seat.

Motorcyles – motorcyclists require helmets.

Snow tyres – studded snow tyres are not allowed.

Alcohol limit – the alcohol limit on drivers is 0.8 per cent, equivalent to two small beers or a quarter of a litre of wine.

Traffic and weather conditions

Are there any hold-ups?
Gibt es Verkehrsstörungen?
gipt es fer-kayrs-stoer-oong-en

Is there a different way to the stadium?
Gibt es eine andere Route zum Stadium?
gipt es yn-e and-er-e root-e tsoom shtad-ee-oom

Is there a toll on this motorway?
Ist diese Autobahn gebührenpflichtig?
ist deez-e owt-o-ban ge-bûr-en-pfleekht-eekh

Traffic and weather conditions

What is causing this traffic jam?
Wodurch wird dieser Stau verursacht?
voa-doorkh virt deez-er shtow fer-oor-zakht

What is the speed limit?
Was ist die Höchstgeschwindigkeit?
vas ist dee hoekst-ge-shvind-eekh-kyt

When is the rush hour?
Wann sind die Stoßzeiten?
van zint dee shtoas-tsyt-en

Is the traffic heavy?
Gibt es viel Verkehr
gipt es feel fer-kayr

Is the traffic one-way?
Ist das eine Einbahnstraße?
ist das yn-e yn-ban-shtras-e

When will the road be clear?
Wann ist die Straße wieder frei?
van ist dee stras-e veed-er fry

Do I need snow chains?
Brauche ich Schneeketten?
browkh-e eekh shnay-ket-en

Is the pass open?
Ist der Paß geöffnet?
ist der pas ge-oef-net

Is the road to Saarbrücken snowed up?
Ist die Strecke nach Saarbrücken verschneit?
*ist dee **shtrek**-e nakh zar-**brük**-en fer-**shnyt***

Parking

There are no yellow lines along the kerbs in Germany. Parking regulations are indicated on road signs.

Where is there a car park?
Wo gibt es hier einen Parkplatz?
*voa gipt es heer yn-en **park**-plats*

Can I park here?
Kann ich hier parken?
*kan eekh heer **park**-en*

Do I need a parking disc?
Brauche ich hier eine Parkscheibe?
***browkh**-e eekh heer yn-e **park**-shyb-e*

Where can I get a parking disc?
Wo kann ich eine Parkscheibe bekommen?
*voa kan eekh yn-e **park**-shyb-e be-**kom**-en*

How long can I stay here?
Wie lange kann ich hier bleiben?
*vee **lang**-e kan eekh heer **blyb**-en*

At the service station

Is it safe to park here?
Kann man hier unbesorgt parken?
kan man heer oon-be-zorgt park-en

What time does the car park / multi-storey car park close?
Wann schließt der Parkplatz / Parkhaus?
van shleest der park-plats / das park-hows

Where do I pay?
Wo kann ich zahlen?
voa kan eekh tsal-en

Do I need coins for the meter?
Brauche ich Münzen für die Parkuhr?
browkh-e eekh mûnts-en fûr dee park-oor

Do I need parking lights?
Brauche ich eine Parkleuchte?
browkh-e eekh yn-e park-loykht-e

At the service station

As part of the anti-pollution effort, most German cars now run on lead-free fuel and leaded petrol is becoming increasingly difficult to find. Super leaded may be phased out by 1998. If you are renting a car, find out which fuel it requires as some cars take diesel. German filling stations are highly competitive and it is worth shopping around for bargains, but

At the service station

not on the *Autobahn*. Self-service (*SB Tanken*) is cheapest.
Pumps marked *bleifrei* contain unleaded fuel.

Do you take credit cards?
Kann ich mit Kreditkarte zahlen?
kan eekh mit kray-deet-kart-e tsal-en

Fill the tank please
Voll bitte
fol bit-e

25 litres of — unleaded petrol
fünf und zwanzig Liter — bleifreies Benzin
fûnf-oont-tsvant-seekh lee-ter — bly-fry-es ben-tseen

— **3 star**
— Normalbenzin
— *nor-mal-ben-tseen*

— **4 star**
— Super
— *soop-er*

— **diesel**
— Diesel
— *deez-el*

Can you clean the windscreen?
Können Sie die Windschutzscheibe putzen?
koen-en zee dee vint-shoots-shyb-e poots-en

Breakdowns and repairs

Check — the oil
Prüfen Sie bitte — den Ölstand
prûf-en zee bit-e — den oel-shtant

— the water
— das Wasser
— das vas-er

Check the tyre pressure please
Bitte prüfen Sie den Reifendruck
bit-e prûf-en zee den ryf-en-drook

The pressure should be 2.3 at the front and 2.5 at the rear
Der Druck sollte vorne zwei Komma drei und hinten zwei
  Komma fünf sein
der drook solt-e forn-e tsvy comma dry oont hint-en tsvy
  comma fûnf zyn

I need some distilled water
Ich brauche destilliertes Wasser
eekh browkh-e de-steel-eert-es vas-er

Breakdowns and repairs

There are three automobile clubs in Germany: ADAC (*Allge-meiner Deutscher Automobil Club*), Am Westpark 8, D-81373 Munich; AvD (*Automobilclub von Deutschland*), Lyonerstrasse 16, D-60528 Frankfurt; DTC (*Deutscher Touring-Automobil Club*), Amalienburgstrasse 23, D-81247

Breakdowns and repairs

Munich. ADAC or AvD operate tow trucks on all motor-ways, and ADAC maintains the *Strassenwachthilfe*, which patrols roads to assist disabled vehicles. There are orange emergency roadside telephones every 3 kilometres (1.8 miles), which are announced by blue *Notruf* (emergency) signs. ADAC will provide road assistance free of charge if the damage can be repaired within half an hour. If not, you will pay repair and towing fees. On minor roads find the nearest phone box, dial 19211 and ask, in English, for road service.

Is there a telephone nearby?
Gibt es hier in der Nähe ein Telefon?
*gipt es heer in der **ne**-e yn **tay**-lay-foan*

Can you send a recovery truck?
Können Sie einen Abschleppdienst senden?
*koen-en zee yn-en **ap**-shlep-deenst **zen**-den*

Can you take me to the nearest garage?
Können Sie mich zur nächsten Werkstatt bringen?
*koen-en zee meekh tsoor **nekst**-en **verk**-shtat **bring**-en*

I have run out of petrol
Ich habe kein Benzin mehr
*eekh **hab**-e kyn ben-**tseen** mayr*

Can you give me a can of petrol, please?
Könnten Sie mir bitte einen Kanister Benzin geben?
*koent-en zee meer **bit**-e yn-en kan-**eest**-er ben-**tseen** gayb-en*

Breakdowns and repairs

Can you give me — a push?
Könnten Sie mich bitte —anschieben?
koent-en zee meekh bit-e — an-sheeb-en

— a tow?
— abschleppen?
— ap-shlep-en

Is there a mechanic here?
Ist ein Mechaniker da?
ist yn me-khan-ee-ker da

Do you have an emergency fan belt?
Haben Sie einen Reservekeilriemen?
hab-en zee yn-en re-zerv-e-kyl-reem-en

Do you have jump leads?
Haben Sie ein Starthilfekabel?
hab-en zee yn shtart-hilf-e-kab-el

Can you find out what the trouble is?
Können Sie feststellen, was das Problem ist?
koen-en zee fest-shtel-en vas das prob-laym ist

There is something wrong
Etwas funktioniert nicht
et-vas foonk-tsee-oa-neert neekht

There is something wrong with the car
Mit dem Auto stimmt etwas nicht
mit dem owt-oa shtimt et-vas neekht

Breakdowns and repairs

Will it take long to repair it?
Würde eine Reparatur lang dauern?
vûrd-e yn-e re-pa-ra-toor lang dow-ern

Is it serious?
Ist es etwas Größeres / Ernsthaftes?
ist es et-vas groes-er-es / ernst-haf-tes

Can you repair it for the time being?
Können Sie es übergangsweise reparieren?
koen-en zee es ûb-er-gangz-vyz-e re-pa-reer-en

Can you replace the windscreen wiper blades?
Können Sie die Scheibenwischergummis ersetzen?
koen-en zee dee shyb-en-vish-er-goom-eez er-zets-en

Can you repair a flat tyre?
Können Sie einen platten Reifen reparieren?
koen-en zee yn-en plat-en ryf-en re-pa-reer-en

Do you have the spare parts?
Haben Sie Ersatzteile?
hab-en zee er-zats-tyl-e

I have a flat tyre
Ich habe einen platten Reifen
eekh hab-e yn-en plat-en ryf-en

I have locked myself out of the car
Ich habe mich aus dem Wagen ausgesperrt
eekh hab-e meekh ows dem vag-en ows-ge-spert

Breakdowns and repairs

I have locked the ignition key inside the car
Ich habe den Zündschlüssel im Auto eingeschlossen
*eekh **hab**-e den **tsûnt**-shlûs-el im **owt**-oa **yn**-ge-shlos-en*

I need a new fan belt
Ich brauche einen neuen Keilriemen
*eekh **browkh**-e yn-en **noy**-en **kyl**-reem-en*

I think there is a bad connection
Ich glaube, da ist ein Wackelkontakt
*eekh **glowb**-e da ist yn **vak**-el-kon-takt*

My car has been towed away
Mein Wagen wurde abgeschleppt
*myn **vag**-en voord-e **ap**-ge-shlept*

My car has broken down
Mein Auto hatte eine Panne
*myn **owt**-o hat-e yn-e **pan**-e*

My car will not start
Mein Wagen springt nicht an
*myn **vag**-en **shpring**t **neekht** an*

My windscreen has cracked
Meine Windschutzscheibe ist gesprungen
*myn-e **vint**-shuts-shyb-e ist ge-**shproong**-en*

The air-conditioning does not work
Die Klimaanlage funktioniert nicht
*dee **klee**-ma-an-lag-e **foonk**-tsee-oa-neert neekht*

The battery is flat
Die Batterie ist leer
*de bat-e-**ree** ist **layr***

  The engine — has broken down
  Der Motor — ist kaputt
*der **moa**-toar — ist ka-**poot***

      — is overheating
      — ist überhitzt
      *— ist **ûb**-er-**hitst***

The exhaust pipe has fallen off
Der Auspuff ist abgefallen
*der **ows**-poof ist **ap**-ge-fal-en*

There is a leak in the radiator
Die Kühlung ist undicht
*dee **kûl**-oong ist **oon**-deekht*

Accidents and the police

Although German police officers are polite and businesslike, they are not to be messed with. If you fail to treat an officer with the proper respect, you may receive an on-the-spot fine. Not many of them speak more than a bit of English. Germans are very law-abiding, so beware of petty offences, which are subject to fines and will mark you out as a foreigner (for instance, littering or ignoring the red light at a pedestrian

Accidents and the police

crossing, even if there are no people in sight). There are two emergency numbers that are common to all areas: 110 for accidents and police, 112 for fire services.

There has been an accident
Ein Unfall ist passiert
*yn **oon**-fal ist pa-**seert***

We must call — an ambulance
  Wir müssen — den Notarzt rufen
  *veer **mûs**-en — den **noat**-artst **roof**-en*

  — the police
  — die Polizei rufen
  *— dee pol-ee-**tsy** **roof**-en*

What is your name and address?
Was sind Ihr Name und Ihre Adresse?
*vas zint eer **nam**-e oont eer-e a-**dress**-e*

You must not move
Sie dürfen sich nicht bewegen
*zee **dûrf**-en zeekh neekht be-**vayg**-en*

I could not stop in time
Ich konnte nicht rechtzeitig zum Stehen kommen
*eekh **kont**-e neekht **rekht**-tsyt-eekh tsoom **shtay**-en **kom**-en*

I did not know about the speed limit
Ich wußte nichts von der Geschwindigkeitsbegrenzung
*eekh **voost**-e neekhts fon der ge-**shvind**-eekh-kyts-be-**grents**-oong*

104

I did not see the bicycle
Ich habe das Fahrrad nicht gesehen
eekh hab-e das far-rat neekht ge-zay-en

He did not stop
Er hat nicht angehalten
er hat neekht an-ge-halt-en

He is a witness
Er ist Zeuge
er ist tsoyg-e

He overtook on a bend
Er überholte in einer Kurve
er ûb-er-holt-e in yn-er koorv-e

He ran into the back of my car
Er fuhr auf meinen Wagen auf
er foor owf myn-en vag-en owf

He stopped suddenly
Er bremste plötzlich
er bremst-e ploets-leekh

He was moving too fast
Er ist zu schnell gefahren
er ist tsoo shnel ge-far-en

I did not see the sign
Ich habe das Zeichen nicht gesehen
eekh hab-e das tsykh-en neekht ge-zay-en

Accidents and the police

Here are my insurance documents
Hier sind meine Versicherungsunterlagen
heer zint myn-e fer-*seekh*-er-oongs-*oont*-er-lag-en

Here is my driving licence
Da ist mein Führerschein
da ist myn *fûr-er-shyn*

I cannot find my driving licence
Ich kann meinen Führerschein nicht finden
eekh **kan** myn-en *fûr-er-shyn* neekht **find**-en

Do you want my credit card?
Brauchen Sie meine Kreditkarte?
browkh-en zee myn-e kray-*deet*-kart-e

Do you want my passport?
Brauchen Sie meinen Paß?
browkh-en zee myn-en *pas*

I am very sorry. I am a visitor
Es tut mir sehr leid. Ich bin nur zu Besuch hier
es **toot** meer zayr **lyt** eekh bin **noor** tsoo be-**zookh** heer

I did not understand the sign
Ich habe das Zeichen nicht verstanden
eekh **hab**-e das *tsykh*-en neekht fer-**shtand**-en

How much is the fine?
Wie hoch ist die Geldbuße?
vee **hoakh** ist dee **gelt**-boos-e

Accidents and the police

I have not got enough money. Can I pay at the police station?
Ich habe nicht genug Geld. Kann ich bei der Polizeiwache zahlen?
*eekh **hab**-e neekht ge-noog **gelt**. **kan** eekh by der pol-ee-tsy-vakh-e **tsal**-en*

I was only driving at 50 kilometres an hour
Ich bin nur fünfzig Kilometer pro Stunde gefahren
*eekh **bin** noor **fûnf**-tseekh kee-loa-**mayt**-er pro **shtoond**-e ge-**far**-en*

I have not had anything to drink
Ich habe nichts getrunken
*eekh **hab**-e neekhts ge-**troonk**-en*

I was overtaking
Ich habe überholt
*eekh **hab**-e ûb-er-**hoalt***

I was parking
Ich habe geparkt
*eekh **hab**-e ge-**parkt***

That car was too close
Dieser Wagen hielt nicht genügend Abstand
*deez-er **vag**-en heelt **neekht** ge-**nûg**-end **ap**-stand*

The brakes failed
Die Bremsen versagten
*dee **bremz**-en fer-**zagt**-en*

Car parts

The car number was...
Das Nummernschild war...
*das **noom**-ern-shilt var...*

The car skidded
Der Wagen schleuderte
*der **vag**-en **shloyd**-ert-e*

The car swerved
Der Wagen scherte aus
*der **vag**-en **shayrt**-e **ows***

The car turned right without signalling
Der Wagen bog rechts ab, ohne zu blinken.
*der **vag**-en boag **rekhts** ap oan-e tsoo **blink**-en*

The road was icy
Die Straße war vereist
*dee **stras**-e var **fer**-yst*

The tyre burst
Der Reifen platzte
*der **ryf**-en **platst**-e*

Car parts

accelerator
Gaspedal
gas-pay-dal

aerial
Antenne
*an-**ten**-e*

air filter
Luftfilter
looft-filt-er

alternator
Drehstromgenerator
dray-stroam-gay-nay-ra-tor

antifreeze
Frostschutzmittel
frost-shoots-mit-el

automatic gearbox
Automatikschaltung
owt-oa-ma-teek-shalt-oong

axle
Achse
aks-e

battery
Batterie
bat-e-ree

bonnet
Kühlerhaube
kûl-er-howb-e

boot
Kofferraum
kof-er-rowm

brake fluid
Bremsenflüssigkeit
bremz-en-flûs-eekh-kyt

brake light
Bremsleuchte
bremz-loykht-e

brakes
Bremsen
bremz-en

bulb
Glühbirne
glû-birn-e

bumper
Stoßstange
shtoas-shtang-e

car-phone
Autotelefon
owt-oa-tay-lay-foan

carburettor
Vergaser
fer-gas-er

child seat
Kindersitz
kind-er-zits

Car parts

choke
Choke
tshoak

clutch
Kupplung
koop-loong

cooling system
Kühlung
kûl-oong

cylinder
Zylinder
tsû-lind-er

disc brake
Scheibenbremse
shyb-en-bremz-e

distributor
Verteiler
fer-tyl-er

door
Tür
tûr

dynamo
Lichtmaschine
leekht-ma-sheen-e

electrical system
Stromanlage
shtroam-an-lag-e

engine
Motor
moa-toar

exhaust system
Auspuffanlage
ows-poof-an-lag-e

fan belt
Keilriemen
kyl-reem-en

foot pump
Fußpumpe
foos-poomp-e

fuel gauge
Benzinanzeige
ben-tseen-an-tsyg-e

fuel pump
Benzinpumpe
ben-tseen-poomp-e

fuse
Sicherung
zeekh-er-oong

gear box
Gangschaltung
gang-shalt-oong

gear lever
Ganghebel
gang-hayb-el

generator
Generator
gay-nay-ra-tor

hammer
Hammer
ham-er

hand brake
Handbremse
hant-bremz-e

hazard lights
Warnblinkanlage
varn-blink-an-lag-e

headlights
Scheinwerfer
shyn-verf-er

heating system
Heizung
hyts-oong

hood
Haube
howb-e

horn
Hupe
hoop-e

hose
Schlauch
shlowkh

ignition key
Zündungsschlüssel
tsûnd-oongs-shlûs-el

ignition
Zündung
tsûnd-oong

indicator
Blinker
blink-er

jack
Wagenheber
vag-en-hayb-er

lights
Leuchten
loykht-en

Car parts

lock
Schloß
shlos

rear-view mirror
Rückscheibe
rûk-shyb-e

oil filter
Ölfilter
oel-filt-er

reflectors
Reflektoren
reflek-toar-en

oil
Öl
oel

reversing light
Rückfahrscheinwerfer
rûk-far-shyn-verf-er

oil pressure
Ölstand
oel-shtant

roof-rack
Dachgepäckträger
dakh-ge-pek-treg-er

petrol
Benzin
ben-tseen

screwdriver
Schraubenzieher
shrowb-en-tsee-er

points
Anschlüsse
an-shlûs-e

seat belt
Sicherheitsgurt
zeekh-er-hyts-goort

pump
Pumpe
poomp-e

seat
Platz
plats

radiator
Kühlung
kûl-oong

shock absorber
Stoßdämpfer
shtoas-dempf-er

112

silencer
Schalldämpfer
shal-dempf-er

socket set
Steckschlüsselset
shtek-shlûs-el-set

spanner
Schraubenschlüssel
shrowb-en-shlûs-el

spare part
Ersatzteil
er-zats-tyl

spark plug
Zündkerze
tsûnd-kerts-e

speedometer
Geschwindigkeitsmesser
ge-shvind-eekh-kyts-mes-er

starter motor
Anlasser
an-las-er

steering
Lenkung
lenk-oong

steering wheel
Lenkrad
lenk-rat

sun roof
Schiebedach
sheeb-e-dakh

suspension
Federung
fay-der-oong

tools
Werkzeug
verk-tsoyg

towbar
Abschleppstange
ap-shlep-shtang-e

transmission
Getriebe
ge-treeb-e

tyre pressure
Reifendruck
ryf-en-drook

tyre
Reifen
ryf-en

Road signs

warning light
Warnleuchte
varn-loykht-e

water
Wasser
vas-er

wheel
Rad
rat

windscreen
Windschutzscheibe
vint-shoots shyb-e

windshield
Frontscheibe
front-shyb-e

wipers
Scheibenwischer
shyb-en-vish-er

Road signs

bitte rechts fahren
bit-e rekhts far-en
keep to the right

Durchfahrt verboten
doorkh-fart fer-boat-en
no thoroughfare

kein Eingang
kyn-yn-gang
no entry

private Zufahrt
pree-vat-e tsoo-fart
private road

Parken nur für Anwohner
park-en noor für an-voan-er
parking for residents only

Umleitung
oom-lyt-oong
diversion

EATING OUT

Where to eat

There is a great variety in restaurants and eating places, with the most sophisticated and expensive ones usually in the cities. For the most authentic and down-to-earth options, there is a *Gaststätte* in almost every street, and every village has its *Gasthof,* and such establishments are almost as easy to find in the east.

The emphasis in the Gasthof or Gaststätte is on good home cooking – simple food, wholesome rather than refined, at reasonable prices. These are also places where people will meet in the evening for a chat, a beer and a game of cards. They normally serve hot meals from 11.30am to 9 or 10pm, but many places stop serving between 2 and 6pm except for cold snacks.

Lunch rather than dinner is the main meal of the day in Germany, followed by *Abendbrot* or *Abendessen* (supper) in the evening. Coffee and cake are still often enjoyed in the afternoon, and some bakeries (*Konditorei*) double as cafés for this purpose. It is also perfectly acceptable to visit a Gaststätte or Gasthof for just a pot of coffee outside the busy lunch hour.

To save money in the cities, consider dining in restaurants

Reservations

serving foreign cuisine. Germany has a vast number of moderately priced Turkish, Italian, Greek, Chinese and Balkan restaurants.

Unpretentious restaurants expect you to seat yourself. In traditional restaurants the waiter is addressed as 'Herr Ober', waitresses as 'Fräulein' ('Miss' – the address of Fräulein is no longer acceptable in other situations, since there is now no distinction made between married and single women).

A number of fast food chains exist all over Germany, including McDonald's, Pizza Hut, Burger King, Wienerwald (chicken) and Nordsee fish bars. However, the small takeaway kiosks or snack bars (*Imbiss*) selling *Bratwurst* (fried or grilled sausage), *Bockwurst* (frankfurter) and *Pommes frites* (chips) are still popular. Sometimes you find butcher shops (*Metzgerei*) serving warm snacks on their premises.

Reservations

Should we reserve a table?
Sollten wir einen Tisch bestellen?
*sollt-en veer yn-en **tish** be-shtel-en*

Can I book a table for four at 8 o'clock?
Kann ich für acht Uhr einen Tisch für vier Personen
  buchen?
*kan eekh fûr **akht** oor yn-en **tish** fûr **feer** per-zoan-en
  bookh-en*

Useful questions

Can we have a table for four?
Könnten wir bitte einen Tisch für vier Personen haben?
koent-en veer bit-e yn-en tish fûr feer per-zoan-en hab-en

I am a vegetarian
Ich bin Vegetarier
eekh bin veg-e-ta-reer-er

We would like a table — by the window
Wir hätten gerne einen Tisch — am Fenster
verr het-en gern-e yn-en tish — am fenst-er

— **on the terrace**
— auf der Terrasse
— *owf der te-ras-e*

Useful questions

Do you have a local speciality?
Haben Sie eine Spezialität des Ortes?
hab-en zee yn-e shpe-tsee-a-lee-tet des ort-es

Do you have a set menu?
Haben Sie ein Menü
hab-en zee yn me-nû

Do you have yoghurt?
Haben sie Joghurt?
hab-en zee yoa-goort

117

EATING OUT

Useful questions

What do you recommend?
Was können Sie empfehlen?
vas koen-en zee emp-fayl-en

What is the dish of the day?
Was ist das Gericht des Tages?
vas ist das ge-reekht des tag-es

What is the soup of the day?
Was ist die Tagessuppe?
vas ist dee tag-es-zoop-e

What is this called?
Wie heißt das?
vee hyst das

What is this dish like?
Wie schmeckt dieses Gericht?
vee shmekt deez-es ge-reekht

Which local wine do you recommend?
Welchen hiesigen Wein empfehlen Sie?
velkh-en heez-ig-en vyn emp-fayl-en zee

How do I eat this?
Wie esse ich das?
vee es-e eekh das

Are vegetables included?
Ist das Gemüse inbegriffen?
ist das ge-mûz-e in-be-grif-en

Is the local wine good?
Ist der hiesige Wein gut?
*ist der **heez**-ig-e **vyn** goot*

Is this cheese very strong?
Ist das ein sehr kräftiger Käse?
*ist das yn zayr **kreft**-eg-er **kez**-e*

Is this good?
Ist das gut?
*ist das **goot***

Ordering your meal

I will take the set menu
Ich nehme das Menü
*eekh **naym**-e das me-**nû***

The menu, please
Die Karte, bitte
*dee **kart**-e **bit**-e*

I will take that
Ich nehme das
*eekh **naym**-e das*

That is for me
Das ist für mich
*das ist **fûr meekh***

Ordering your meal

Can we start with soup?
Können wir mit einer Suppe anfangen?
koen-en veer mit yn-er zoop-e an-fang-en

I will have salad
Ich hätte gerne einen Salat
eekh het-e gern-e yn-en za-lat

Could we have some butter?
Könnten wir etwas Butter haben?
koent-en veer et-vas boot-er hab-en

Can we have some bread?
Können wir Brot haben?
koen-en veer broat hab-en

I like my steak — very rare
Ich bevorzuge mein Steak — sehr wenig durchgebraten
eekh be-foar-tsoog-e myn stayk — zayr vayn-eekh doorkh-ge-brat-en

— medium rare
— mittel
— mit-el

— rare
— nicht sehr stark durchgebraten
— neekht zayr shtark doorkh-ge-brat-en

— **well done**
— durchgebraten
— *doorkh-ge-brat-en*

Could we have some more bread, please?
Könnten wir bitte noch etwas Brot haben?
koent-en veer bit-e nokh et-was broat hab-en

Can I see the menu again, please?
Kann ich bitte die Karte noch einmal sehen?
kan eekh bit-e dee kart-e nokh yn-mal zay-en

Ordering drinks

The wine list, please
Die Weinkarte bitte
dee vyn-kart-e bit-e

We will take the Riesling
Wir nehmen den Riesling
veer naym-en den reez-ling

A bottle of house red wine, please
Eine Flasche roten Hauswein, bitte
yn-e flash-e roat-en hows-vyn bit-e

A glass of dry white wine, please
Ein Glas trockenen Weißwein, bitte
yn glas trok-en-en vys-vyn bit-e

Ordering drinks

Another bottle of red wine, please
Noch eine Flasche Rotwein, bitte
nokh yn-e flash-e roat-vyn bit-e

Another glass, please
Noch ein Glas, bitte
nokh yn glas bit-e

Black coffee, please
Schwarzen Kaffee, bitte
shvarts-en ka-fay bit-e

Coffee with milk, please
Kaffee mit Milch, bitte
ka-fay mit milkh bit-e

Some plain water, please
Könnten wir bitte etwas Leitungswasser haben?
koent-en veer bit-e et-was lyt-oongs-vas-er hab-en

Can we have some mineral water?
Können wir Mineralwasser haben?
koen-en veer min-er-al-vas-er hab-en

Two beers, please
Zwei Bier, bitte
tsvy beer bit-e

Paying the bill

German restaurateurs are very accommodating when it comes to splitting the bill and paying separately, and waitresses in small establishments often add up individual bills at the table. Tipping in Germany is purely voluntary (up to 10 per cent of the total bill) and indicates your particular satisfaction with the service you have received.

Can we have the bill, please?
Könnten wir bitte die Rechnung haben?
koent-en veer bit-e dee rekh-noong hab-en

Can I have an itemized bill?
Könnte ich bitte eine spezifizierte Rechnung haben?
koent-e eekh bit-e yn-e shpets-ee-fee-tseert-e rekh-noong hab-en

Do you accept traveller's cheques?
Nehmen Sie Reiseschecks?
naym-en zee ryz-e-sheks

Is service included?
Ist die Bedienung im Preis inbegriffen?
ist dee be-deen-oong im prys in-be-grif-en

Is tax included?
Ist die Steuer mitinbegriffen?
ist dee shtoy-er mit-in-be-grif-en

Paying the bill

Is there any extra charge?
Gibt es zusätzliche Gebühren?
*gipt es **tsoo**-zets-leekh-e ge-**bûr**-en*

Can I have a receipt?
Könnte ich bitte eine Quittung haben?
*koent-e eekh bit-e yn-e **kvit**-oong **hab**-en*

I would like to pay with my credit card
Ich möchte mit meiner Kreditkarte zahlen
*eekh **moekht**-e mit myn-er kray-**deet**-kart-e **tsal**-en*

I do not have enough currency
Ich habe nicht genug Landeswährung
*eekh hab-e **neekht** ge-noog **land**-es-ver-oong*

This is not correct
Das stimmt nicht
*das **shtimt** neekht*

This is not my bill
Das ist nicht meine Rechnung
*das ist neekht **myn**-e **rekh**-noong*

You have given me the wrong change
Sie haben mir falsch herausgegeben
*zee **hab**-en meer **falsh** hayr-**ows**-ge-gayb-en*

Complaints and compliments

This is cold
Das ist kalt
*das ist **kalt***

This is not what I ordered
Das ist nicht, was ich bestellt habe
*das ist **neekht** vas eekh be-**shtellt hab**-e*

Waiter! We have been waiting for a long time
Herr Ober! Wir warten jetzt schon sehr lange
*her **oab**-er veer **vart**-en yetst shoan zayr **lang**-e*

The meal was excellent
Das Essen war ausgezeichnet
*das **es**-en var **ows**-ge-tsykh-net*

This is excellent
Das ist ausgezeichnet
*das ist **ows**-ge-tsykh-net*

Can I have the recipe?
Könnte ich bitte das Rezept haben?
*koent-e eekh bit-e das re-**tsept** hab-en*

125

Food

Nowadays Germany has a large number of good ethnic restaurants in larger towns and cities, but if your taste runs more towards meat and potatoes rather than tofu and yoghurt, you will find the food in Germany hearty and satisfying. Be careful when you order from a German menu if you don't speak the language, because ingredients like eel, blood sausage and brains are not uncommon. But don't let this deter you from taking risks – they are often tastier than you think.

The typical German breakfast (*Frühstück*) consists of coffee or tea with rolls or bread, jam, cold meat and cheese, sometimes boiled eggs. Lunch (*Mittagessen*) as the main meal of the day can consist of a variety of hot meals, usually with meat, potatoes and vegetables or salad. *Eintopf* can be found on menus of traditional restaurants. It is a hearty stew cooked in one pot, as the name indicates, often containing meat, vegetables, potatoes and beans. Supper (*Abendbrot* or *Abendessen*) is a re-enactment of breakfast with a wider choice of meat and cheese and often accompanied by beer.

German bread (*Brot*) is of astounding quality and variety. *Vollkornbrot* is whole-wheat, which has a different meaning in Germany. *Schwarzbrot* (black bread) is dense, dark and slightly acidic and *Roggenbrot* is rye bread. *Brötchen* are rolls, which also come in different shapes and styles. Many Germans indulge in the ritual of *Kaffee und Kuchen* (*see* page 115), which is a fourth meal taken in the afternoon.

Food

In addition to bread, the staples of the German diet are *Wurst* (sausage in various shapes and sizes), *Schweinefleisch* (pork), *Rindfleisch* (beef), *Kalbfleisch* (veal), *Kartoffeln* (potatoes) and *Eier* (eggs). Dairy products include cheese and butter and especially *Schlagsahne* (whipped cream).

To sample local specialities as you travel around Germany is to appreciate the diversity of its food. Everyone has heard of *Sauerkraut* (pickled cabbage) or *Sauerbraten* (pickled beef), but there is much more to German cuisine. In Bavaria there are various kinds of *Knödel* (potato dumplings with fillings) and *Weisswurst,* which is a sausage made with milk. In Swabia and Baden there are *Spätzle* (noodles) and *Maultaschen* ('pasta pockets'). *Pfannekuchen* (pancakes) are universal, while *Kaiserschmarren*, a southern version, are pancakes chopped up and served with powdered sugar, raisins and sometimes boiled fruit. Hessians do amazing things with potatoes, and in the northern regions you can enjoy the tradition of a *Kohl und Pinkelfahrt*. This usually involves a long walk on a bitterly cold day, accompanied by some warming *Schnaps* and culminating at a rural inn, where a large meal of *Kohl* (kale), *Kasseler* (smoked pork) and *Pinkel* (sausage containing offal and cereal) is consumed, with more *Schnaps*. Because of the fishing industry, fish specialities are popular in the north. Herring used to be cheap and is still used in a variety of ways, either fried (*Brathering*), pickled in different ways (*Matjeshering, Bismarckhering*), rolled and pickled (rollmops), in salads (*Heringsalat*) and in many other ways.

Menu reader

Ananas
an-an-as
pineapple

Äpfel
ep-fel
apples

Apfelkompott
ap-fel-kom-pot
apple compote

Apfelkuchen
ap-fel-kookh-en
apple cake

Apfelpüree / Apfelmus
ap-fel-pû-re / ap-fel-moos
apple sauce

Aprikosen
ap-ree-koaz-en
apricots

Artischocken
ar-tee-shoak-en
artichoke

Aubergine
oa-ber-zheen-e
aubergine

Austern
owst-ern
oysters

Avocado
a-voa-ka-doa
avocado

Backhuhn / Brathuhn
bak-hoon / brat-hoon
baked/roasted chicken

Bananen
ba-na-nen
bananas

Barbe
barb-e
mullet

Basilikum
ba-zee-lee-koom
basil

Beefsteak
beef-stayk
beefsteak

belegtes Brot
be-laygt-es broat
cold sandwich

Birne
birn-e
pear

Biskuitkuchen
bees-kveet-kookh-en
sponge cake

Blaue Zipfel
blow-e tsip-fel
sausages cooked with
vinegar and onions
(Franconia)

Blumenkohl
bloom-en-koal
cauliflower

Blut- und Leberwurst
bloot oont layb-er-woorst
black pudding and liver
sausage (Franconia)

Bohneneintopf
boan-en-yn-topf
bean stew

Bratapfel
brat-ap-fel
baked apple

Brathuhn / Backhuhn
brat-hoon / bak-hoon
fried / breaded chicken

Bratkartoffeln
brat-kar-tof-eln
roast potatoes

Brötchen
broet-khen
bread rolls

Brunnenkresse
broon-en-kres-e
watercress

Butter
boot-er
butter

Champignoncremesuppe
sham-peen-yoang-kraym-zoop-e
cream of mushroom soup

129

Menu reader

Champignons mit Knoblauch
sham-peen-yoans mit knoab-lowkh
mushrooms with garlic

Champignons mit Soße
sham-peen-yoans mit zoas-e
mushrooms in sauce

Chicorée
shee-koa-ray
chicory

Cornichon
kor-nee-shoang
gherkin

Creme Caramel
kraym ka-ra-mel
crème caramel

Datteln
dat-eln
dates

Dessert
de-sert
pudding

dünne Pfannkuchen/ Crêpes
dûn-e pfan-kookh-en/krep
thin pancakes

　　— mit Marmelade
　　— mit mar-me-lad-e
　　— with jam

　　— mit Schokolade
　　— mit shok-oa-lad-e
　　— with chocolate

Eier mit Schinken
y-er mit shink-en
eggs with ham

Eier mit Speck
y-er mit shpek
eggs with bacon

Eiernudeln
y-er-nood-eln
egg noodles

einfaches Kotelett
yn-fakh-es ko-te-let
plain cutlet

eingelegte Makrele
yn-ge-laygt-e mak-rayl-e
marinated mackerel

130

Eiskrem
ys-kraym
ice cream

Ente
ent-e
duck

Erbsen
erp-sen
peas

Erbsensuppe
erp-sen-soop-e
pea soup

Erdbeeren
ert-bayr-en
strawberries

Erdbeeren mit Sahne
ert-bayr-en mit zan-e
strawberries with cream

Essig
es-eekh
vinegar

Estragon
es-tra-gon
tarragon

Fasan
fa-zan
pheasant

Filet
fee-lay
steak fillet

Fisch
fish
fish

Fleisch
flysh
meat

Fleisch vom Grill
flysh fom gril
grilled meats

Flußkrebs
floos-krayps
crayfish

Forelle
fo-rel-e
trout

Forelle blau
fo-rel-e blow
boiled trout

131

Menu reader

Forelle gebraten
fo-rel-e ge-brat-en
fried trout

französische Bohnen
fran-tsoe-zeesh-e boan-en
French beans

Gaisburger Marsch
gys-boorg-er marsh
stew with pasta and potatoes

Gans
gans
goose

gebratene Froschschenkel
ge-brat-en-e frosh-shenk-el
fried frog legs

gefüllter Hase
ge-fûl-ter haz-e
stuffed rabbit

gemischter Salat
ge-misht-er za-lat
mixed salad

Gemüse
ge-mûz-e
vegetables

Gemüsecremesuppe
ge-mûz-e-kraym-zoop-e
cream of vegetable soup

Granatäpfel
gra-nat-ep-fel
pomegranates

Grapefruit / Pampelmuse
grayp-froot / pam-pel-mus-e
grapefruit

grüne Paprika
grûn-e pap-ree-ka
green pepper (vegetable)

grüner Pfeffer
grûn-er pfef-er
green pepper (spice)

Gurke
goork-e
cucumber

Gurkensalat
goork-en-za-lat
cucumber salad

Halve Hahn
halv-e han
cheese roll (Cologne)

Haxe (Lammshaxe)
haks-e (lams-hax-e)
leg (of lamb, etc)

Hechtfilet
hekht-fee-lay
hake fillet

Himbeeren
him-bayr-en
raspberries

Hühnerbrühe
hûn-er-brû-e
chicken broth

Hühnereintopf
hûn-er-yn-topf
chicken stew

Hühnersuppe
hûn-er-zoop-e
chicken soup

Hummer
hoom-er
lobster

Joghurt
yoa-goort
yoghurt

Kalbskotelett
kalps-ko-te-let
veal cutlet

Karotten
ka-rot-en
carrots

Kartoffelpüree
kar-tof-el-pû-ray
mashed potatoes

Kartoffelsalat
kar-to-fel-za-lat
potato salad

Käsekuchen
kez-e-kookh-en
cheese cake

Kerbel
ker-bel
chervil

Kirschen
kirsh-en
cherries

Knoblauch
knoab-lowkh
garlic

Menu reader

Knödel / Klöße
knoed-el / kloes-e
dumplings

Kohl / Weißkohl
koal / vys-koal
cabbage

Kopfsalat
kopf-za-lat
lettuce

Krapfen
krapf-en
doughnuts

Kuchen
kookh-en
cake

Pastete
pas-tay-tuh
pie

Kürbis
kûr-bees
squash

Kutteln
koot-eln
tripe

Lamm am Spieß
lam am shpees
lamb on the spit

Lammkotelett
lam-kot-e-let
lamb cutlet

Lammshaxe
lams-hax-e
leg of lamb

Lauch
lowkh
leeks

Lauchsuppe
lowkh-zoope
leek soup

Leberkäse
layb-er-kez-e
processed meat (Bavaria)

Lorbeerblätter
loar-bayr-blet-er
bayleaf

Mais
ma-ees
sweet corn

Maissalat
ma-ees-za-lat
corn salad

Makrele
mak-rayl-e
mackerel

Mandelkuchen
mand-el-kookh-en
almond cake

marinierter Fisch
ma-ree-neert-er fish
marinated fish

Markkürbis
mark-kûr-bis
marrow

Marmelade
mar-me-lad-e
jam

Maultaschen
mowl-tash-en
pasta filled with spinach and
chopped meat

Melone
me-loan-e
melon

Miesmuscheln
meez-moosh-eln
mussels

Milchreis
milkh-rys
rice pudding

Minze
mints-e
mint

Mousse au Chocolat
moos oa sho-koa-la
chocolate mousse

Muscheln
moosh-eln
clams

Niereneintopf
neer-en-yn-topf
stewed kidney

Nudeln
nood-eln
pasta

Obst mit Schlagsahne
obst mit shlag-zan-e
fruit with whipped cream

135

Menu reader

Obstsalat
obst-za-lat
fruit salad

Ochse am Spieß
oks-e am shpees
ox on the spit

Öl
oel
oil

Oliven
o-leev-en
olives

Orangen / Apfelsinen
o-ranzh-en / ap-fel-zeen-en
oranges

Palatschinken
pa-lat-shink-en
Austrian pancakes

Pasternake
past-er-nak-e
parsnip

Petersilie
payt-er-zeel-ee-e
parsley

Pfirsich
pfir-zeekh
peach

Pflaumen
pflowm-en
plums

Pilze / Champignons
pilts-e / sham-peen-yoans
mushrooms

Pommes frites
pom freet
French fries

Pumpernickel
poomp-er-nik-el
wholemeal bread

Radieschen
ra-dees-khen
radishes

Räucherschinken
roykh-er-shink-en
cured ham

Reineclauden
ryn-e-kload
greengages

Rindereintopf
rind-er-yn-topf
beef stew

Rindsbrühe
rints-brû-e
beef broth

Rosenkohl
roaz-en-koal
Brussels sprouts

Rosmarin
roaz-mar-reen
rosemary

Rote Bete
roat-e bayt-e
beetroot

rote Paprika
roat-e pap-ree-ka
red pepper

Rote-Bohnen-Suppe
rot-e-boan-en-zoop-e
kidney-bean soup

Rühreier
rûr-y-er
scrambled eggs

russischer Salat
roos-eesh-er za-lat
Russian salad

Salat
za-lat
lettuce

Salbei
zal-by
sage

Sardinen
zar-deen-en
sardines

Sauerkraut
zow-er-krowt
pickled white cabbage

Saumagen
zow-mag-en
pork and processed meat

Scampi
skamp-ee
scampi

Schalotten
sha-lot-en
shallots

Menu reader

Schinkenbrot
shink-en-broat
ham sandwich

Spaghetti
shpa-get-ee
spaghetti

Schmorbraten
shmoar-brat-en
braised beef

Spanferkel
shpan-ferk-el
suckling pig on the spit

Schnittbohnen
shnit-boan-en
broad beans

Spargel
shparg-el
asparagus

Schnittlauch
shnit-lowkh
chives

Spiegeleier
shpeeg-el-y-er
eggs sunny side up

schwarze Johannisbeeren
shvarts-e joa-han-is-bayr-en
blackcurrants

Spinat
spi-nat
spinach

Schweinebraten
shvyn-e-brat-en
pork roast

Squash
skwosh
squash

Schweinskotelett
shvyns-ko-te-let
pork cutlet

Staudensellerie
shtowd-en-zel-er-ee
celery

Soße mit grünem Pfeffer
zoas-e mit grün-em pfef-er
green pepper sauce

Tafelspitz mit Kren
taf-el-spits mit krayn
beef and horseradish

Thunfisch
toon-fish
tuna

Thymian
tûm-ee-an
thyme

Tintenfisch
tint-en-fish
cuttlefish

Tintenfisch
tint-en-fish
squid

Tomaten
toa-mat-en
tomatoes

Tomatensalat
*toa-mat-en-za-la*t
tomato salad

Tomatensoße
toa-mat-en-zoas-e
tomato sauce

Tomatensuppe
toa-mat-en-zoop-e
tomato soup

Trauben
trowb-en
grapes

Truthahn
troot-han
turkey

Vanillesauce
va-neel-e-zoas-e
custard

vom Grill
fom gril
grilled/barbecued

Wassermelone
vas-er-me-loan-e
watermelon

weichgekochtes Ei
vykh-ge-kokht-es y
soft boiled egg

Weinsoße
vyn-zoas-e
wine sauce

weiße Rüben
vys-e rûb-en
turnip

Drinks

Würstchen
vûrst-khen
sausage

Zitrone
tsee-troan-e
lemon

Zitronenbaiserkuchen
tsee-troan-en-be-zay-kookh-en
lemon meringue

Zucchini
tsoo-kee-nee
courgettes

Zuckererbsen
tsook-er-erps-en
sweet peas

Zunge
tsoong-e
tongue

Zwiebel
tsveeb-el
onion

Zwiebelsoße
tsveeb-el-zoas-e
onion sauce

Drinks

Beer

Germans have been brewing beer since the eighth century, but in the Middle Ages the lucrative trade of the monastic orders was taken over by the lords of the land.

The variety of German beers is astonishing. *Vollbier* contains 4 per cent alcohol, *Export* 5 per cent, *Bockbier* 6.25 per cent and *Doppelbock* should be reserved for special occasions. There are also different colours, *ein Helles* being of a standard light colour, while *ein Dunkles* could be as dark as

Wines and spirits

Coca-Cola. *Pils* is popular in the north, *Weissbier* in the south, *Kölsch* in Cologne and *Altbier* in Dusseldorf. *Fassbier* is a draught straight from the barrel.

Venues for drinking beer vary. There are *Biergärten* (beer garden) and *Bierkeller* (the indoor version meaning beer cellar). Many *Gaststätten* have a *Stammtisch* (locals' table) for their regular visitors, who sit around this table playing cards while drinking.

Wines and spirits

Although Germans are known to consume vast quantities of beer, they also produce some excellent wines in various famous wine growing areas. The main concentrations of viniculture lie around the Rhine and Mosel valleys, the Main River, Franconia and Baden-Baden. Rhine wine bottles are brown, all others are green, and the Franconian wines may be bottled in the characteristically shaped *Boxbeutel*.

Most German wines are white, but they vary a lot in sweetness and alcohol content. The cheapest are called *Tafelwein* (table wine), while *Qualitätswein* (quality wine) is better and *Qualitätswein mit Prädikat* (quality wine with distinction) is even superior. *Prädikat* wines are further subdivided according to the ripeness of grapes at harvest time: *Kabinett, Spätlese, Auslese, Beerenauslese* or *Trockenbeerenauslese*.

The most famous grapes grown in Germany arc *Riesling, Muller-Thurgau* and *Traminer,* which produces the *Gewürztraminer.* In wine-growing areas, the thirsty traveller can

Drinks reader

stop at a *Weinstube* to sample the local produce. Many places celebrate annual wine festivals.

After a meal, many Germans aid their digestion by throwing back a *Schnaps* distilled from barley (*Korn*) or various fruit-like cherries (*Kirschwasser*), plums (*Zwetschgenwasser* or *Sliwowitz*), raspberries (*Himbeergeist*) and apricots (*Aprikosenlikör*). A popular strong-tasting herb liqueur is called *Jagermeister*.

If you order water (*Wasser*) in a restaurant you will be given mineral water. Tap water is called *Leitungswasser*, which Germans would find odd to drink with a meal.

Drinks reader

Apfelsaft
ap-fel-zaft
apple juice

Aprikosensaft
ap-ree-koz-en-zaft
apricot juice

Bananenmilch
ba-na-nen-milkh
banana milkshake

Bier
beer
beer

Bierflasche / Flaschenbier
beer-flash-e / flash-en-beer
bottled beer

Bowle
bow-le
punch

Calvados
kal-va-dos
apple brandy

Cappuccino
ka-poo-tshee-no
cappuccino

Champagner / Sekt
*sham-**pan**-yer / zekt*
champagne

Cidre / Apfelwein
*seedr / **ap**-fel-vyn*
cider

Cola
koal-a
coke

Dosenbier
doaz-en-beer
canned beer

ein Glas Rotwein
*yn glas **roat**-vyn*
a glass of red wine

ein Glas Weißwein
*yn glas **vys**-vyn*
a glass of white wine

ein großes Bier
*yn gros-es **beer***
a large beer

ein Kännchen Kaffee
*yn **ken**-khen ka-fay*
small pot of coffee

ein Weinbrand
*yn **vyn**-brant*
a brandy

eine Tasse Kaffee
*yn-e **tas**-e ka-fay*
a cup of coffee

Eiskaffee
ys-ka-fay
iced coffee

entkoffeinierter Kaffee
*ent-ko-fee-**neert**-er ka-fay*
decaffeinated coffee

Grog
grog
tea with rum

Kaffee
ka-fay
coffee

Kaffee mit Milch
*ka-fay mit **milkh***
coffee with milk

Kaffee mit Milch
*ka-fay mit **milkh***
white coffee

Drinks reader

Kamillentee
ka-meel-en-tay
camomile tea

Likör
lee-koer
liqueur

Limonade
lee-mo-nad-e
lemonade

löslicher Kaffee
loes-leekh-er ka-fay
instant coffee

Mineralwasser
mee-ner-al-vas-er
mineral water

Orangengetränk
o-ranzh-en-ge-trenk
orange drink

Orangensaft
o-ranzh-en-zaft
orange juice

Pfirsichsaft
pfir-zeekh-zaft
peach juice

Pharisäer
fa-reez-e-er
coffee with rum and cream

Roséwein
roa-zay-vyn
rosé wine

Rum
room
rum

Schnaps
shnaps
liquor

Sodawasser
zoad-a-vas-er
soda

Starkbier
shtark-beer
stout

Tee mit Milch
tay mit milkh
tea with milk

Tee mit Zitrone
tay mit tsee-troan-e
lemon tea

144

Tonic Wasser
ton-ik vas-er
tonic water

Wermut
vayr-moot
vermouth

Traubensaft
trowb-en-zaft
grape juice

Whisky
whisk-ee
whisky

OUT AND ABOUT

The weather

Germany's climate is predominantly mild and temperate, but there are regional variations. Cold snaps can plunge the temperatures well below freezing, particularly in the Alps, which makes winter sports possible from December to March. Regular snow and frost is also common in inland regions and the hills of the Harz, the Black Forest, Lower Saxony and Franconia. Summers are usually sunny and warm, although you should be prepared for some cloudy and wet days. Seasonal temperature differences are more pronounced in southern regions, while the north is kept temperate by the vicinity of the North Sea. Near the Alps, particularly in higher regions, the summer often starts late. Autumn can be warm and soothing. A peculiar weather condition called *Föhn* can be experienced in southern parts. This is a warm Alpine wind, often associated with atmospheric pressure changes, which may cause headaches for some people. Average summer temperatures range from 20°C to 30°C. The average winter temperature is 0°C.

Is it going to get any warmer?
Wird es wärmer werden?
*virt es **verm**-er vayrd-en*

Is it going to stay like this?
Wird es so bleiben?
*virt es zo **blyb**-en*

Is there going to be a thunderstorm?
Wird es ein Gewitter geben?
*wirt es yn ge-**vit**-er gayb-en*

Isn't it a lovely day?
Ist es nicht ein wunderschöner Tag?
*ist es neekht yn **voond**-er-shoen-er **tag***

It has stopped snowing
Es hat aufgehört zu schneien
*es hat **owf**-ge-hoert tsoo **shny**-en*

It is a very clear night
Es ist eine sehr klare Nacht
*es ist yn-e **zayr** klar-e **nakht***

It is far too hot
Es ist viel zu heiß
*es ist **veel** tsoo **hys***

It is foggy
Es ist neblig
*es ist **nay**-bel-eekh*

The weather

It is going — to be fine
 Es wird — schön
 es virt — shoen

> **— to be windy**
> — windig
> *— vind-eekh*

> **— to rain**
> — regnen
> *— rayg-nen*

> **— to snow**
> — schneien
> *— shny-en*

It is raining again
Es regnet wieder
es rayg-net veed-er

It is very cold
Es ist sehr kalt
es ist zayr kalt

It is very windy
Es ist sehr windig
es ist zayr vind-eekh

There is a cool breeze
Es geht ein kühler Wind
es gayt yn kûl-er vint

What is the temperature?
Welche Temperatur haben wir?
velkh-e tem-per-a-toor hab-en veer

Will it be cold tonight?
Wird es heute nacht kalt werden?
virt es hoyt-e nakht kalt vayr-den

Will the weather improve?
Wird das Wetter besser werden?
virt das vet-er bes-er vayrd-en

Will the wind die down?
Wird sich der Wind legen?
virt zeekh der vint layg-en

On the beach

Western mainland beaches often consist of grass bordering onto mudflats, but there are beautiful sandy beaches on the East and North Frisian Islands, which are easily accessible by regular ferry services.

Local authorities often charge a fee for the use of beaches, and on the islands you can hire a *Strandkorb* (wicker beach seat). Because currents around the islands can be treacherous, bathers should stick to the areas designated for swimming. Taking a walk on exposed mudflats can be quite spectacular and is supposed to be healthy, but beware of getting trapped on banks by the incoming tide. In the east there are

On the beach

spectacular chalk cliffs on the coast at the island of Rügen and there are many sandy beaches on the Baltic coast and islands.

Can you recommend a quiet beach?
Können Sie einen ruhigen Strand empfehlen?
koen-en zee yn-en roo-eeg-en shtrant emp-fayl-en

Is it safe to swim here?
Kann man hier unbesorgt schwimmen?
kan man heer oon-be-zorgt shvim-en

Is the current strong?
Ist die Strömung stark?
ist dee stroem-oong shtark

Is the sea calm?
Ist das Meer ruhig?
ist das mayr roo-eekh

Is the water warm?
Ist das Wasser warm?
ist das vas-er varm

Is there a lifeguard here?
Gibt es hier einen Bademeister?
gipt es heer yn-en bad-e-myst-er

Can we change here?
Können wir uns hier umziehen?
koen-en veer oons heer oom-tsee-en

Is it possible to go — sailing?
    Kann man hier — segeln — gehen?
    kan man heer — ***sayg-*** eln gay-en

          — surfing?
          — Wellenreiten?
          — ***vel-*** en-ryt-en

          — water skiing?
          — Wasserski fahren?
          — ***vas-*** er-shee-far-en

          — wind surfing?
          — Windsurfen
          — ***vint-*** surf-en

Is this beach private?
Ist das ein Privatstrand?
*ist das yn pree-**vat**-shtrant*

When is high tide?
Wann ist Flut?
*van ist **floot***

When is low tide?
Wann ist Ebbe?
*van ist **eb**-e*

Sport and recreation

Among the popular sports in Germany are fishing, tennis, swimming, water sports, hiking and rock climbing, winter sports and cycling. Germany's lakes and rivers have a variety of fish including carp, pike, eel, bream, zander and trout, but you need a licence and a local permit to fish in the open season. Tennis courts can be found in virtually all major tourist spots, where you can usually hire rackets.

There are plenty of heated outdoor and indoor swimming pools in the country in addition to swimming beaches on lakes and seaside resorts, where water sports facilities can also be found. Germany has 180 yachting schools along the coast and on major inland lakes. There is a network of hiking routes in the lowlands and highlands for rambling and rock-climbing enthusiasts, and the Alpine region offers plenty of opportunity for winter sports.

Many resorts offer bicycles for hire and so do the railways. In urban areas the bike can be one of the most efficient ways of getting around. Because it is regarded as a form of transport rather than of recreation, towns and cities are well equipped with designated cycle lanes, sometimes in the street, sometimes on the pavement. For touring purposes, good maps and routes are available from ADFC-Bundesverband, Postfach 10 77 47, D-28077 Bremen.

Sport and recreation

Is there a heated swimming pool?
Haben Sie ein beheiztes Schwimmbecken?
hab-en zee yn be-hytst-es shvim-bek-en

Can I rent — a sailing boat?
  Kann ich — ein Segelboot — mieten?
  kan eekh — yn zayg-el-boat meet-en

         — a rowing boat?
         — ein Ruderboot?
         — yn rood-er-boat

Can I rent the equipment?
Kann ich die Ausrüstung mieten?
kan eekh dee ows-rûst-oong meet-en

        Can we — play tennis?
  Können wir — Tennis spielen?
koen-en veer — te-nees shpeel-en

         — play golf?
         — Golf spielen?
         — golf shpeel-en

         — play volleyball?
         — Volleyball spielen?
         — vo-lay-bal shpeel-en

Can we go riding?
Können wir Reiten gehen?
koen-en veer ryt-en gay-en

Entertainment

Where can we fish?
Wo können wir fischen?
voa koen-en veer fish-en

Do we need a permit?
Brauchen wir eine Lizenz?
browkh-en veer yn-e lee-tsents

Entertainment

Germans call their country the land of *Dichter und Denker* (poets and philosophers), and indeed Germany's cultural legacy is rich, richer almost than that of any other nation in Europe. This international inheritance extends to the visual arts, music, architecture, literature and film. Opportunities for an evening's entertainment are virtually limitless. Whether it is a pub, cinema, theatre, concert, disco or something entirely different, most cities have a lot to offer.

Is there — a disco?
Gibt es hier — eine Disco?
gipt es heer — yn-e disk-oa

— a casino?
— ein Kasino?
— *yn ka-see-noa*

— a theatre?
— ein Theater?
— *yn tay-a-ter*

154

— **a good nightclub?**
— einen guten Nachtclub?
— *yn-en goot-en **nakht**-kloob*

Are there any films in English?
Werden hier auch englische Filme gezeigt?
vayrd**-en heer owkh **eng**-leesh-e **film**-e ge-**tsygt

How much is it per person?
Wieviel kostet es pro Person?
vee-feel** **kost**-et es pro per-**zoan

How much is it to get in?
Wieviel kostet es hineinzugehen?
vee-feel **kost**-et es heen-**yn**-tsoo -gay-en

Is there a reduction for children?
Gibt es eine Ermäßigung für Kinder?
***gipt** es yn-e er-**mes**-eeg-oong für **kind**-er*

Two stall tickets, please
Zwei Karten für Sperrsitze, bitte / Zwei Karten im Parkett, bitte
*tsvy **kart**-en für **shper**-sits-e bit-e / tsvy **kart**-en im par-ket bit-e*

Two tickets, please
Zwei Karten, bitte
*tsvy **kart**-en bit-e*

Sightseeing

On many inland waters in Germany there are river-boat and motorboat services available, and very often rail passes are valid for boat trips too. In addition to connecting towns within Germany, there are passenger and car ferries operating to offshore islands in the North and Baltic Sea. KD Rhine Line offers a programme of luxury cruises along the Rhine, Main, Mosel, Neckar, Saar, Elbe and Danube rivers. During the summer there are good services between Bonn and Koblenz as well as Koblenz and Bingen. Other cruises are offered on the Oder, Saale and Weser. Boat trips are very popular and advance booking is advisable.

Are there any boat trips on the river?

Gibt es Bootsfahrten auf dem Fluß?

*gipt es **boats**-fart-en owf dem **floos***

Are there any guided tours of the castle?

Gibt es Führungen durch die Burg?

*gipt es **fûr**-oong-en doorkh dee **boorg***

Are there any guided tours?

Gibt es Führungen?

*gipt es **fûr**-oong-en*

Is there a tour of the cathedral?

Gibt es eine Führung durch den Dom?

*gipt es yn-e **fûr**-oong doorkh den **doam***

Is there an English-speaking guide?
Haben Sie einen Englisch sprechenden Führer?
hab-en zee yn-en eng-leesh shprekh-end-en fûr-er

How long does the tour take?
Wie lange dauert die Rundfahrt?
vee lang-e dow-ert dee roont-fart

When is the bus tour?
Wann findet die Busrundfahrt statt?
van find-et dee boos-roont-fart shtat

What is there to see here?
Was gibt es hier zu sehen?
vas gipt es heer tsoo zay-en

What is this building?
Was für ein Gebäude ist das?
vas fûr yn ge-boyd-e ist das

When was it built?
Wann wurde es gebaut?
van voord-e es ge-bowt

Can we go in?
Können wir hineingehen?
koen-en veer heen-yn-gay-en

Is it open to the public?
Ist es für die Öffentlichkeit zu betreten?
ist es fûr dee oef-ent-leekh-kyt tsoo be-trayt-en

Sightseeing

Is there a guidebook?
Haben Sie einen Ortsführer?
*hab-en zee yn-en **orts**-fûr-er*

What is the admission charge?
Was kostet der Eintritt?
*vas **kost**-et der **yn**-tritt*

How much is it for a child?
Wieviel kostet es für ein Kind?
*vee-feel **kost**-et es fûr yn **kint***

When is the bus tour?
Wann findet die Busrundfahrt statt?
*van **find**-et dee **boos**-roont-fart **shtat***

Can we go up to the top?
Können wir nach oben gehen?
***koen**-en veer nakh **oab**-en gay-en*

Is this the best view?
Ist das die beste Aussicht?
*ist das dee **best**-e **ows**-zeekht*

What time does the gallery open?
Wann öffnet die Galerie?
*van **oef**-net dee gal-e-**ree***

Can I take photos?
Können wir Fotos machen?
***koen**-en veer **foa**-toas **makh**-en*

158

Can I use flash?
Kann ich mein Blitzlicht verwenden?
*kan eekh myn **blits**-leekht fer-**vend**-en*

Souvenirs

Where can I buy postcards?
Wo kann ich Postkarten kaufen?
*voa kan eekh **post**-kart-en **kowf**-en*

Where can we buy souvenirs?
Wo kann ich Andenken kaufen?
*voa kan eekh **an**-denk-en **kowf**-en*

Have you got an English guidebook?
Haben Sie einen Führer in englischer Sprache?
***hab**-en zee yn-en **fûr**-er in **eng**-leesh-er **shprakh**-e*

Have you got any colour slides?
Haben Sie Farbdias?
***hab**-en zee **farb**-dee-as*

Going to church

In Germany, the church and the state are separate and there is complete religious freedom. Three-quarters of all Germans claim a Christian faith, half belonging to the Roman Catholic

Going to church

Church and half to the Protestant branch of the church (*Evangelische Kirche*) that was based on the teachings of Martin Luther. Other Christian denominations are also active, including predominantly the Evangelical Free Church, Baptists, Old Catholics and Quakers. There are distinct Catholic and Protestant areas in Germany, the north being predominantly Protestant, while southern areas and the Rhineland tend to be Catholic. With the arrival of ethnic minorities, Islamic and Orthodox cultures are growing, and there are also some Jewish communities.

I would like to see — a priest
    Ich möchte — einen Priester — sehen,
*eekh **moekht**-e — yn-en **preest**-er **zay**-en*

        — a minister
        — einen Pfarrer
        *yn-en **pfar**-er*

        — a rabbi
        — einen Rabbiner
        *yn-en ra-**been**-er*

Where is the — Catholic church?
    Wo ist die — katholische Kirche?
*voa ist dee — ka-**toal**-eesh-e **kirkh**-e*

        — Baptist church?
        — Baptistenkirche?
        *— bap-**teest**-en-**kirkh**-e*

— **mosque?**
— Moschee?
— *mo-shay*

— **Protestant church?**
— evangelische Kirche?
— *ay-fan-gay-lish-e kirkh-e*

— **synagogue?**
— Synagoge?
— *zû-na-goag-e*

What time is the service?
Wann findet der Gottesdienst statt?
van find-et der got-es-deenst shtat

SHOPPING

General information

Business hours vary and are detailed under Getting Around (*see* page 67). On Sunday most shops are closed, apart from bakeries (for fresh bread and cake), florists (if invited to a private house, fresh flowers are a traditional present for your host) and newsagents. Shops also close on public holidays (*see* page 227). Most towns and city centres have their pedestrian shopping precincts with department stores, boutiques, hairdressers', pharmacies, butchers, bakers, cafés and specialist shops. Some old towns still have their weekly markets.

Outside the centres there are supermarkets, DIY stores, car showrooms, carpet warehouses and petrol stations. World-famous shopping centres are the Kurfürstendamm in Berlin, the Königsallee in Düsseldorf, the Hansequarter in Hamburg and the Zeil in Frankfurt/Main. Watch out for the 'Tax-free' sign, where you will receive a tax-free cheque with your purchase. This will need a stamp at the check-in at the start of your homeward journey.

When buying souvenirs or gifts, most shops will offer to gift-wrap your purchase.

General phrases and requests

How much is this?
Was macht das?
*vas **makht** das*

How much does that cost?
Was kostet das?
*vas **kost**-et das*

  How much is it — per kilo?
  Wieviel kostet es — pro Kilo?
*vee-feel **kost**-et es — pro **keel**-oa*

              — per metre?
              — pro Meter?
              *— pro **mayt**-er*

I like this one
Das gefällt mir
*das ge-**felt** meer*

I do not like it
Das gefällt mir nicht
*das ge-**felt** meer **neekht***

I will take that one
Ich nehmen das
*eekh **naym**-e das*

General phrases and requests

I will take the other one
Ich nehmen das andere
*eekh **naym**-e das and-er-e*

I will take this one
Ich nehmen dieses
*eekh **naym**-e deez-es*

No, the other one
Nein, das andere
*nyn das **and**-er-e*

Have you got anything cheaper?
Haben Sie etwas Billigeres?
*hab-en zee et-vas **bil**-ig-er-es*

Can I have a carrier bag?
Könnte ich eine Tragetasche haben?
***koent**-e eekh yn-e **trag**-e-tash-e hab-en*

Can I pay for air insurance?
Kann ich gegen Gebühr eine Luftfrachtversicherung
  abschließen?
*kan eekh gayg-en ge-**bûr** yn-e **looft**-frakht-fer-zeekh-er-
  oong **ap**-shlees-en*

Can I see that one over there?
Könnte ich mir das da drüben ansehen?
***koent**-e eekh meer das da -**drûb**-en **an**-zay-en*

General phrases and requests

Can I see that umbrella?
Könnte ich mir diesen Schirm anschauen?
koent-e eekh meer deez-en **shirm an**-show-en

Can you deliver to my hotel?
Können Sie es mir in meinem Hotel liefern?
*koen-en zee es meer in myn-em hoa-**tel leef**-ern*

Do you sell sunglasses?
Verkaufen Sie Sonnenbrillen?
*fer-**kowf**-en zee **zon**-en-bril-en*

I am looking for a souvenir
Ich suche ein Andenken
*eekh **zookh**-e yn **an**-denk-en*

I do not have enough money
Ich habe nicht genug Geld
*eekh hab-e **neekht** ge-noog- **gelt***

Please forward a receipt to this address
Bitte schicken Sie eine Rechnung an diese Adresse
*bit-e **shik**-en zee yn-e **rekh**-noong an **deez**-e a-**dres**-e*

Will you send it by air freight?
Schicken Sie es per Luftfracht?
*shike-en zee es per **looft**-frakht*

Please pack it for shipment
Bitte packen Sie das für den Transport ein
*bit-e **pak**-en zee das für den trans-**port** yn*

General phrases and requests

Please wrap it up for me
Bitte packen Sie es mir ein
*bit-e **pak**-en zee es meer **yn***

There is no need to wrap it
Einzupacken ist nicht nötig
*yn-tsoo-pak-en ist neekht **noet**-eekh*

We need to buy some food
Wir müssen etwas zu essen kaufen
*veer **mûs**-en et-vas tsoo **es**-en **kowf**-en*

What is the total?
Was macht das zusammen?
*vas **makht** das tsoo-**zam**-en*

Where can I buy some clothes?
Wo kann ich Kleidung kaufen?
***voa** kan eekh **kly**-doong **kowf**-en*

Where can I buy cassette tapes and compact discs?
Wo kann ich Tonbandkassetten und Compact Disks kaufen?
***voa** kan eekh **toan**-bant-ka-**set**-en oont kom-**pakt** disks
  kowf-en*

Where can I buy tapes for my camcorder?
Wo kann ich Kassetten für meinen Camcorder kaufen?
***voa** kan eekh ka-**set**-en fûr myn-en **kam**-kord-er **kowf**-en*

Where can I get my camcorder repaired?
Wo kann ich meinen Camcorder reparieren lassen?
***voa** kan eekh myn-en **kam**-kord-er re-pa-**reer**-en las-en*

Where is the children's department?
Wo ist die Kinderabteilung?
voa ist *dee* **kind**-er-ap-tyl-oong

Where is the the food department?
Wo ist die Lebensmittelabteilung?
voa ist *dee* **layb**-ens-mit-el-**ab**-tyl-oong

Buying groceries

You can buy all your groceries under one roof at a supermarket, but you might prefer small shops with a wider choice. The displays in bakeries (*Bäckerei* for bread, *Konditorei* more for pastry and cakes) are astounding and mouth-watering. The butcher's is called *Metzgerei* or *Schlachterei,* where you will find a large variety of fresh and cooked meats and sausages. The greengrocer's is *Obst- und Gemüsehandlung,* where produce is usually very fresh and plentiful. *Lebensmittel* are general groceries.

Can I please have — some sugar?
    Kann ich bitte — etwas Zucker — haben?
    kan eekh bit-e — et-vas **tsook**-er — **hab**-en

    — a bottle of wine?
    — eine Flasche Wein?
    — yn-e flash-e **vyn**

Buying groceries

— **a kilo of sausages?**
— ein Kilo Würste?
— *yn keel-oa **vûrst-e***

— **a leg of lamb?**
— eine Lammshaxe?
— *yn-e **lams**-haks-e*

— **a litre of milk?**
— einen Liter Milch?
— *yn-en leet-er **milkh***

— **two steaks?**
— zwei Steaks?
— *tsvy **stayks***

— **a kilo of potatoes?**
— ein Kilo Kartoffeln?
— *yn **keel**-oa kar-tof-eln*

— **a bar of chocolate?**
— eine Tafel Schokolade?
— *yn-e **taf**-el shok-oa-**lad**-e*

Can I please have — **5 slices of ham?**
Kann ich bitte — fünf Scheiben Schinken — haben?
***kan** eekh bit-e* — *fûnf **shyb**-en **shink**-en— **hab**-en*

— **100 grams of ground coffee?**
— hundert Gramm gemahlenen Kaffee?
— *hoond-ert **gram** ge-mal-en-en **ka**-fay?*

— **half a dozen eggs?**
— ein halbes Dutzend Eier?
— *yn halb-es **doots**-ent y-er?*

— **half a kilo of butter?**
— ein halbes Kilo Butter?
— *yn halb-es **keel**-oa **boot**-er?*

Groceries

baby food
Babynahrung
***bayb**-ee-nar-oong*

biscuits
Kekse
***kayk**-se*

bread
Brot
broat

butter
Butter
***boot**-er*

cheese
Käse
***kez**-e*

coffee
Kaffee
***ka**-fay*

cream
Sahne
***zan**-e*

eggs
Eier
***y**-er*

flour
Mehl
mayl

groceries
Lebensmittel
***layb**-enz-mit-el*

Groceries

jam
Marmelade
mar-me-lad-e

rice
Reis
rys

margarine
Margarine
mar-ga-reen-e

salt
Salz
zalts

milk
Milch
milkh

soup
Suppe
zoop-e

mustard
Senf
zenf

sugar
Zucker
tsook-er

oil
Öl
oel

tea
Tee
tay

pasta
Nudeln
nood-eln

vinegar
Essig
es-eekh

pepper
Pfeffer
pfef-er

yoghurt
Joghurt
yoa-goort

Meat and fish

beef
Rindfleisch
rint-flysh

chicken
Huhn
hoon

cod
Kabeljau
kab-el-yow

fish
Fisch
fish

hake
Hecht
hekht

ham
Schinken
shink-en

herring
Hering
hayr-ing

kidneys
Nieren
neer-en

lamb
Lamm
lam

liver
Leber
layb-er

meat
Fleisch
flysh

mussels
Muscheln
moosh-eln

pork
Schweinefleisch
shvyn-e-flysh

sole
Seezunge
zay-tsoong-e

171

At the newsagent's

tuna
Thunfisch
toon-fish

veal
Kalbsfleisch
kalps-flysh

At the newsagent's

These usually sell tobacco, too, and are often situated in tiny premises or kiosks. Germans are avid newspaper readers and virtually every city has its own daily newspaper. These are supplemented by a number of major national papers and a wide selection of magazines. In the major cities you can buy all the important international newspapers and periodicals.

Do you have — English newspapers?
Haben Sie — englische Zeitungen?
hab-en zee — eng-leesh-e tsyt-oong-en

— **English books?**
— englische Bücher?
— eng-leesh-e bûkh-er

— **postcards?**
— Postkarten?
— post-kart-en

Do you sell — English paperbacks?
Verkaufen Sie — englische Taschenbücher?
fer-kowf-en zee — eng-leesh-e tash-en-bûkh-er

— **coloured pencils?**
— Farbstifte?
— *farb-shtift-e*

— **drawing paper?**
— Zeichenpapier?
— *tsykh-en-pa-peer*

— **felt pens?**
— Filzschreiber?
— *filts-shryb-er*

— **street maps?**
— Stadtpläne?
— *shttat-plen-e*

I would like — **some postage stamps**
Ich hätte gerne — ein paar Briefmarken
eekh het-e gern-e — *yn par **breef**-mark-en*

— **a bottle of ink**
— einen Behälter mit Tinte
— *yn-en be-**helt**-er mit **tint**-e*

— **a pen**
— einen Federhalter
— *yn-en **fayd**-er-halt-er*

— **a pencil**
— einen Bleistift
— *yn-en **bly**-shtift*

At the tobacconist's

— some adhesive tape
— etwas Klebstreifen
— *etvas **klayb**-shtryf-en*

— some envelopes
— Umschläge
— *__oom__-shleg-e*

I need — some writing paper
Ich brauche — Schreibpapier
*eekh **browkh**-e — **shryb**-pa-peer*

— a local map
— einen Stadtplan
— *yn-en **shtat**-plan*

— a road map
— eine Straßenkarte
— *yn-e **shtras**-en-kart-e*

At the tobacconist's

I would like — a box of matches
Ich hätte gerne — eine Packung Streichhölzer
*eekh het-e gern-e — yn-e **pak**-oong **shtrykh**-hoelts-er*

— a cigar
— eine Zigarre
— *yn-e **tsee**-gar-e*

174

At the tobacconist's

— a cigarette lighter
— ein Feuerzeug
— *yn foy-er-tsoyg*

— a gas (butane) refill
— eine Nachfüllpackung Butangas
— *yn-e nakh-fûl-pak-oong boo-tan-gas*

— a pipe
— eine Pfeife
— *yn-e pfyf-e*

— a pouch of pipe tobacco
— ein Päckchen Pfeifentabak
— *yn pek-khen pfyf-en-ta-bak*

— some pipe cleaners
— ein paar Pfeifenreiniger
— *yn par pfyf-en-ryn-eeg-er*

Do you have cigarette papers?
Haben Sie Zigarettenpapier?
hab-en zee tsee-ga-ret-en-pa-peer

Do you have rolling tobacco?
Haben Sie Tabak zum Selberdrehen?
hab-en zee ta-bak tsoom zelb-er-dray-en

Have you got any American brands?
Führen Sie amerikanische Marken?
fûr-en zee a-may-ree-ka   n-eesh-e mark-en

At the chemist's

Have you got any English brands?
Führen Sie englische Marken?
*fûr-en zee **eng**-leesh-e **mark**-en*

A packet of ... please
Bitte eine Packung ...
*bit-e yn-e **pak**-oong...*

— with filter tips
— mit Filter
— *mit **filt**-er*

— without filters
— ohne Filter
— *oan-e **filt**-er*

At the chemist's

Dispensing chemists are called *Apotheke,* where you can buy medicines and take your doctor's prescription. A *Drogerie* is a drugstore, which sells cosmetics, soap, toothpaste and the like as well as over-the-counter remedies. Both are open during normal business hours. There are notices with information about night-time and Sunday services.

I need some high-protection suntan cream
Ich brauche Sonnencreme mit hohem Schutzfaktor
*eekh browkh-e **zon**-en-kraym-e mit **hoa**-em **shoots**-fak-tor*

At the chemist's

I need some antibiotics
Ich brauche Antibiotika
*eekh **browkh**-e an-tee-bee-o-tee-ka*

Can you give me something for a headache?
Können Sie mir etwas gegen Kopfschmerzen geben?
*koen-en zee meer et-vas gayg-en **kopf**-shmerts-en **gayb**-en*

Can you give me something for a cold?
Können Sie mir etwas gegen eine Erkältung geben?
*koen-en zee meer et-vas gayg-en yn-e er-**kelt**-oong **gayb**-en*

Can you give me something for a cough?
Können Sie mir etwas gegen Husten geben?
*koen-en zee meer et-vas gayg-en **hoost**-en **gayb**-en*

Can you give me something for a sore throat?
Können Sie mir etwas gegen Halsentzündung geben?
*koen-en zee meer et-vas gayg-en **hals**-ent-tsûnd-oong **gayb**-en*

Can you give me something for an upset stomach?
Können Sie mir etwas gegen eine Magenverstimmung
  geben?
*koen-en zee meer et-vas gayg-en yn-e **mag**-en-fer-shtim-oong
  gayb-en*

Can you give me something for sunburn?
Können Sie mir etwas gegen Sonnenbrand geben?
*koen-en zee meer et-vas gayg-en **zon**-en-brant **gayb**-en*

At the chemist's

Can you give me something for chapped lips?
Können Sie mir etwas gegen aufgesprungene Lippen
  geben?
*koen-en zee meer et-vas gayg-en **owf**-ge-shproong-en-e **lip**-en
  gayb-en*

Can you give me something for swollen feet?
Können Sie mir etwas gegen geschwollene Füße geben?
*koen-en zee meer et-vas gayg-en ge-**shvol**-en-e **fûs**-e **gayb**-en*

Can you give me something for toothache?
Können Sie mir etwas gegen Zahnschmerzen geben?
*koen-en zee meer et-vas gayg-en **tsan**-shmerts-en **gayb**-en*

Can you give me something for insect bites?
Können Sie mir etwas gegen Insektenstiche geben?
*koen-en zee meer et-vas gayg-en in-**zekt**-en-shtikh-e **gayb**-en*

Do I need a prescription?
Brauche ich dafür ein Rezept?
browkh**-e eekh da-**fûr** yn re-**tsept

How many do I take?
Wieviel nehme ich davon?
*vee-feel **naym**-e eekh da-**fon***

How often do I take them?
Wie oft nehme ich sie?
*vee oft **naym**-e eekh **zee***

Are they safe for children to take?
Können sie auch bedenkenlos Kindern gegeben werden?
koen-en zee owkh be-***denk***-en-loas ***kind***-ern ge-***gayb***-en
vayrd-en

Do you have toothpaste?
Haben Sie Zahnpasta?
hab-en zee **tsan**-past-a

Medicines and toiletries

aftershave
Rasierwasser
*ra-**zeer**-vas-er*

antihistamine
Antihistamin
ant-ee-his-ta-meen*

antiseptic
Antiseptikum
ant-ee-**zep**-tee-koom*

aspirin
Aspirin
*as-pee-**reen***

Band-aid
Pflaster
pflast-er*

bandage
Verband
*fer-**bant***

bubble bath
Schaumbad
showm-bat*

cleansing milk
Reinigungsmilch
ryn-ee-goongs-milkh*

contraceptive
Empfängnisverhütungsmittel
*emp-**feng**-nis-fer-hût-oongs-
mit-el*

cotton wool
Watte
vat-e*

179

Medicines and toiletries

deodorant
Deodorant
day-oad-oa-rant

Kleenex
Tempo
temp-oa

disinfectant
Desinfektionsmittel
dayz-in-fek-tsee-oans-mit-el

laxative
Abführmittel
ap-fûr-mit-el

eau de Cologne
Eau de Cologne
oa de ko-lon-ye

lipstick
Lippenstift
lip-en-shtift

eye shadow
Lidschatten
leed-shat-en

mascara
Wimperntusche
vim-pern-toosh-e

hair spray
Haarspray
har-shpray

mouthwash
Mundspülung
moont-shpûl-oong

hand cream
Handcreme
hant-kraym

nail file
Nagelfeile
nag-el-fyl-e

hay fever
Heuschnupfen
hoy-shnup-fen

nail varnish
Nagellack
nag-el-lak

insect repellent
Insektenspray
in-zekt-en-shpray

nail varnish remover
Nagellackentferner
nag-el-lak-ent-fern-er

perfume
Parfüm
par-fûm

powder
Puder
pood-er

razor blades
Rasierklingen
ra-zeer-kling-en

sanitary towels
(Hygiene)binden
(hûg-ee-ayn-e) bind-en

shampoo
Haarshampoo
haar-sham-poo

shaving cream
Rasiercreme
ra-zeer-kraym

skin moisturiser
Feuchtigkeitscreme
foykht-eekh-kyts-kraym

soap
Seife
zyf-e

suntan oil
Sonnenöl
zon-en-oel

talc
Puder
pood-er

toilet water
Eau de Toilette
oa de twa-let

toothpaste
Zahnpasta
tsan-past-a

Shopping for clothes

Generally, Germans dress informally, especially in the summer. Even visits to the theatre do not require special dress. The spirit of the age tends towards a conservative elegance

Shopping for clothes

with plenty of scope for individual taste and style. Only in casinos are jacket and tie mandatory while in many discos jeans and trainers are taboo.

I am just looking, thank you
Danke, ich schaue mich nur um
dank-e eekh show-e meekh noor oom

I like it
Es gefällt mir
es ge-felt meer

I do not like it
Es gefällt mir nicht
es ge-felt meer neekht

I would like — this hat
Ich hätte gerne — diesen Hut
eekh het-e gern-e — deez-en hoot

— this suit
— diesen Anzug
— *deez-en an-tsoog*

I like — this one
Mir gefällt — dieses
meer ge-felt — deez-es

— that one there
— das da
— *das da*

182

Shopping for clothes

> **— the one in the window**
> — das im Fenster
> — *das im **fenst**-er*

I will take it
Ich nehme es
*eekh **naym**-e es*

Can I change it if it does not fit?
Kann ich es umtauschen, falls es nicht paßt?
kan** eekh es **oom**-towsh-en fals es neekht **past

Can you please measure me?
Können Sie mich bitte messen?
***koen**-en zee meekh bit-e **mes**-en*

I take continental size 40
In Europa brauche ich Größe 40
*in oy-**roa**-pa browkh-e eekh **groes**-e **feer**-tseekh*

> **Have you got — a large size?**
> Haben Sie eine — größere Größe
> *hab-en zee yn-e — **groes**-er-e **groes**-e*

> **— a smaller size?**
> — kleinere Größe
> *— **klyn**-er-e **groes**-e*

Have you got this in other colours?
Haben Sie das auch in anderen Farben?
***hab**-en zee das owkh in **and**-er-en **farb**-en*

Shopping for clothes

Where are the changing (dressing) rooms?
Wo sind die Umkleidekabinen?
*voa zind dee **oom**-klyd-e-ka-**been**-en*

Where can I try it on?
Wo kann ich es anprobieren?
*voa kan eekh es **an**-pro-beer-en*

Is there a full-length mirror?
Gibt es hier einen großen Spiegel?
*gipt es heer yn-en **groas**-en **shpeeg**-el*

May I see it in daylight?
Kann ich das im Tageslicht anschauen?
*kan eekh das im **tag**-es-likht **an**-show-en*

It does not fit
Es paßt nicht
*es **past** neekht*

Is it too long?
Ist es zu lang?
*ist es tsoo **lang***

Is it too short?
Ist es zu kurz?
*ist es tsoo **koorts***

Is this all you have?
Ist das alles, was Sie haben?
*ist das al-es vas zee **hab**-en*

Shopping for clothes

It does not suit me
Es steht mir nicht
es shtayt meer neekht

    I would like one — with a zip
   Ich hätte gerne eines — mit Reißverschluß
eekh het-e gern-e yn-es — mit rys-fer-shloos

        — without a belt
        — ohne Gürtel
        — oan-e gûrt-e

Is it guaranteed?
Gibt es dafür eine Garantie?
gipt es da-fûr yn-e ga-ran-tee

What is it made of?
Woraus besteht das?
voa-rows be-shtayt das

Is it drip-dry?
Muss man es schleudern?
moos man es shloyd-ern

Is it dry-clean only?
Muß man es chemisch reinigen?
moos man es khaym-eesh ryn-ee-gen

Is it machine-washable?
Kann ich es in der Maschine waschen?
kan eekh es in der mas-sheen-e vash-en

Clothes and accessories

Will it shrink?
Läuft es ein?
loyft es yn

Clothes and accessories

acrylic
Acryl
a-krûl

belt
Gürtel
gûrt-el

blouse
Bluse
blooz-e

bra
BH
bay-ha

bracelet
Armband
arm-bant

brooch
Brosche
broash-e

button
Knopf
knopf

cardigan
Strickjacke
shtrik-yak-e

coat
Mantel
mant-el

corduroy
Cord
kord

denim
Jeansstoff
jeens-shtof

dress
Kleid
klyt

186

Clothes and accessories

dungarees
Latzhose
lats-hoaz-e

jeans
Jeans
jeenz

earrings
Ohrringe
oar-ring-e

jersey
Pulli / Pullover
pool-ee / pool-oav-er

fur
Pelz
pelts

lace
Spitze
shpits-e

gloves
Handschuhe
hant-shoo-e

leather
Leder
layd-er

handbag
Handtasche
hant-tash-e

linen
Leinen
lyn-en

handkerchief
Taschentuch
-en-tookh

necklace
Halskette
hals-ket-e

hat
Hut
hoot

night-dress
Nachthemd
nakht-hemt

jacket
Jacke
yak-e

nylon
Nylon
ny-lon

Clothes and accessories

panties
Unterhosen
oont-er-hoaz-en

pendant
Anhänger
an-heng-er

petticoat
Unterrock
oont-er-rok

polyester
Polyester
pol-ee-est-er

poplin
Popeline
pop-e-leen-e

pullover
Pullover
pool-oav-er

purse
Geldbeutel
gelt-boyt-el

pyjamas
Schlafanzug
shlaf-an-tsoog

raincoat
Regenmantel
rayg-en-mant-el

rayon
Kunstseide/Rayon
koonst-zyd-e/ray-on

ring
Ring
ring

sandals
Sandalen
zan-dal-en

scarf
Schal
shal

shirt
Hemd
hemt

shorts
kurze Hosen / Shorts
koorts-e hoaz-en

silk
Seide
zyd-e

Clothes and accessories

skirt
Rock
rok

swimming trunks
Badehose
bad-e-hoaz-e

slip
Unterrock
oont-er-rok

swimsuit
Badeanzug
bad-e-an-tsoog

socks
Socken
zok-en

T-shirt
T-shirt
tee-shirt

stockings
lange Strümpfe
lang-e shtrûmpf-e

terylene
Terylen
ter-ee-layn

suede
Wildleder
vilt-layd-er

tie
Krawatte / Schlips
kra-vat-e / shlips

suit (men's)
Anzug
an-tsoog

tights
Strumpfhose
shtroompf-hoaz-e

suit (women's)
Kostüm
kos-tûm

towel
Handtuch
hant-tookh

sweater
Pullover
pool-oaf-er

trousers
Hose
hoaz-e

189

Photography

umbrella	**wallet**
Schirm	Brieftasche
shirm	*breef-tash-e*
underpants	**watch**
Unterhose	Armbanduhr
unt-er-hoaz-e	*arm-bant-oor*
velvet	**wool**
Samt	Wolle
zamt	*vol-e*
vest	**zip**
Unterhemd	Reißverschluß
oont-er-hemt	*rys-fer-shloos*

Photography

Can you develop this film, please?
Könnten Sie bitte diesen Film entwickeln?
koent-en zee bit-e deez-en film ent-vik-eln

I would like this photo enlarged
Ich hätte dieses Foto gerne vergrößert
eekh het-e deez-es foa-toa gern-e fer-groes-ert

I would like two prints of this one
Ich hätte gerne zwei Abzüge davon
eekh het-e gern-e tsvy ap-tsûg-e da-fon

When will the photos be ready?
Wann werden die Bilder fertig sein?
van vayrd-en dee bild-er fert-eekh zyn

I need a film — for this camera
Ich brauche einen Film — für diese Kamera
eekh browkh-e yn-en film — fûr deez-e ka-me-ra

— for this camcorder
— für diesen Camcorder
— fûr deez-en kam-kord-er

— for this cine camera
— für diese Filmkamera
— fûr deez-e film-ka-me-ra

— for this video camera
— für diese Videokamera
— fûr deez-e vid-e-oa-ka-me-ra

I want — a black and white film
Ich möchte — einen Schwarzweißfilm
eekh moekht-e — yn-en shvarts-vys-film

— a colour print film
— einen Farbbildfilm
— yn-en farb-bilt-film

— a colour slide film
— einen Farbdiafilm
— yn-en farb-dee-a-film

Camera repairs

    — **batteries for the flash**
    — Batterien für den Blitz
    — *bat-e-**ree**-en für den **blits***

Camera repairs

I am having trouble with my camera
Ich habe Probleme mit meiner Kamera
*eekh hab-e prob-**laym**-e mit myn-er **ka**-mer-ra*

The film is jammed
Der Film klemmt
*der **film** klemt*

There is something wrong with my camera
Mit meiner Kamera stimmt etwas nicht
*mit myn-er **ka**-me-ra **shtimt** et-vas **neekht***

Can you repair it?
Können Sie es reparieren?
*koen-en zee es re-pa-**reer**-en*

Where can I get my camera repaired?
Wo kann ich meine Kamera reparieren lassen?
*voa kan eekh myn-e **ka**-me-ra re-pa-**reer**-en **las**-en*

Camera parts

accessory
Zusatzteil
tsoo-zats-tyl

blue filter
Blaufilter
blow-filt-er

camcorder
Camcorder
kam-kord-er

cartridge
Patrone
pa-troan-e

cassette
Kassette
ka-set-e

cine camera
Filmkamera
film-ka-me-ra

distance
Entfernung
ent-fern-oong

enlargement
Vergrößerung
fer-groes-er-oong

exposure
Belichtung
be-leekht-oong

exposure meter
Belichtungsmesser
be-leekht-oongs-mes-er

flash
Blitz
blits

flash bulb
Blitzlichtbirne
blits-leekht-birn-e

flash cube
Blitzlichtwürfel
blits-leekht-vûrf-el

focal distance
Entfernung
ent-fern-oong

Camera parts

focus
Brennpunkt
bren-poonkt

image
Abbildung
ap-bild-oong

in focus
scharf eingestellt
sharf yn-ge-shtelt

lens cover
Linsendeckel
linz-en-dek-el

lens
Linse
linz-e

negative
Negativ
nay-ga-teef

out of focus
nicht scharf eingestellt
neekht sharf yn-ge-stelt

over-exposed
zu stark belichtet
tsoo shtark be-leekht-et

picture
Bild
bilt

print
Papierbild
pa-peer-bilt

projector
Projektor
proa-yek-tor

red filter
Rotfilter
roat-filt-er

reel
Spule
shpool-e

rewind mechanism
Rückspulmechanismus
rûk-shpool-may-kha-neez-moos

shade
Schatten
shat-en

shutter
Blende
blend-e

194

At the hairdresser's

shutter speed
Belichtungszeit
be-leekht-oongs-tsyt

under-exposed
zu wenig belichtet
tsoo vayn-eekh be-leekht-et

slide
Dia
dee-a

viewfinder
Sucher
zookh-er

transparency
Transparenz
trans-pa-rents

wide-angle lens
Weitwinkelobjektiv
vyt-vink-el-ob-yek-teef

tripod
Stativ
shta-teef

yellow filter
Gelbfilter
gelp-filt-er

At the hairdresser's

I would like to make an appointment
Ich möchte mich anmelden
eekh moekht-e meekh an-meld-en

    I would like — a perm
  Ich hätte gerne — eine Dauerwelle
eekh het-e gern-e — yn-e dow-er-vel-e

        — a blow-dry
        — Föhnen
        — foen-en

At the hairdresser's

> **— my hair dyed**
> — Haare Färben
> — *har-e ferb-en*

> **— my hair streaked**
> — Strähnchen
> — *stren-khen*

> **— shampoo and cut**
> — Waschen und Schneiden
> — *vash-en oont shnyd-en*

> **— shampoo and set**
> — Waschen und Legen
> — *vash-en oont layg-en*

I want a haircut
Ich möchte meine Haare schneiden lassen
eekh moekht-e myn-e har-e shnyd-en las-en

I want a trim
Ich möchte meine Haare nachschneiden lassen
eekh moekht-e myn-e har-e nakh-shnyd-en las-en

> **Please cut my hair — short**
> Schneiden Sie meine Haare bitte — kurz
> *shnyd-en zee myn-e har-e bit-e — koorts*

> **— fairly short**
> — ziemlich kurz
> — *tseem-leekh koorts*

196

At the hairdresser's

> **— in a fringe**
> — zu einem Pony
> — *tsoo yn-em poan-ee*

> **— not too short**
> — nicht allzu kurz
> — *neekht al-tsoo koorts*

Take a little more off the back
Schneiden Sie hinten bitte noch etwas weg
shnyd-en zee hint-en bit-e nokh et-vas vek

Not too much off
Nicht zu viel weg
neekht tsoo feel vek

> **I would like — a conditioner**
> Ich hätte gerne — Conditioner
> *eekh het-e gern-e — kon-dish-en-er*

> **— hair spray**
> — Haarspray
> — *har-shpray*

That is fine, thank you
Das ist gut so, danke
das ist goot zoa dank-e

The dryer is too hot
Die Trockenhaube ist zu heiß
dee trok-en-howb-e ist tsoo hys

Laundry

The water is too hot
Das Wasser ist zu heiß
*das **vas**-er ist tsoo **hys***

Laundry

Is there a launderette nearby?
Gibt es in der Nähe einen Waschsalon?
*gipt es in der **ne**-e yn-en **vash**-za-loan*

How does the machine work?
Wie funktioniert dieses Gerät?
*vee foonk-tsee-o-**neert** deez-es ge-**ret***

How long will it take?
Wie lange dauert das?
*vee lang-e **dow**-ert das*

I will come back in an hour
Ich komme in einer Stunde
*eekh **kom**-e in yn-er **shtoond**-e*

What time do you close?
Wann schließen Sie?
*van **shlees**-en zee*

Can you — clean this skirt?
Können Sie — diesen Rock reinigen?
***koen**-en zee — **deez**-en **rok ryn**-ee-gen*

— **clean and press these shirts?**
— diese Hemden reinigen und bügeln?
— *deez-e **hemd**-en **ryn**-ee-gen oont **bûg**-eln*

— **wash these clothes?**
— diese Kleider waschen?
— *deez-e **klyd**-er **vash**-en*

This stain is — **oil**
Das ist ein — Ölfleck
*das ist yn — **oel**-flek*

— **blood**
— Blutfleck
— ***bloot**-flek*

— **coffee**
— Kaffeefleck
— ***ka**-fay-flek*

— **ink**
— Tintenfleck
— ***tint**-en-flek*

I will come back later
Ich komme später zurück
*eekh kom-e **shpet**-er tsoo-**rûk***

When will I come back?
Wann soll ich zurückkommen?
***van** zol eekh tsoo-**rûk**-kom-en*

General repairs

When will my things be ready?
Wann sind meine Sachen fertig?
*van zint myn-e zakh-en **fert**-eekh*

Can you do it quickly?
Können Sie es schnell machen?
***koen**-en zee es **shnel** makh-en*

Please send it to this address
Bitte schicken Sie es an diese Adresse
*bit-e **shik**-en zee es an deez-e a-**dres**-e*

General repairs

This is — broken
Das ist — kaputt
*das ist — ka-**poot***

    — damaged
    — beschädigt
    *— be-**shed**-eekht*

    — torn
    — zerrissen
    *— tser-**ris**-en*

Can you repair it?
Können Sie es reparieren?
***koen**-en zee es re-pa-**reer**-en*

Have you got a spare part for this?
Haben Sie ein Ersatzteil dafür?
hab-en zee yn er-zats-tyl da-fûr

Would you have a look at this please?
Könnten Sie sich das bitte einmal anschauen?
koent-en zee zeekh das bit-e yn-mal an-show-en

Here is the guarantee
Hier ist die Garantie
heer ist dee ga-ran-tee

I need new heels on these shoes
Ich brauche an diesen Schuhen neue Absätze
eekh browkh-e an deez-en shoo-en noy-e ap-zets-e

At the post office

The post office symbol is a black post-horn on a yellow background. and mailboxes and post vans are all yellow. Opening times for post offices are as under Getting Around (*see* page 67). In small villages the post office may be run from a home and opening times may vary. At stations and airports post offices often stay open longer than normal and may even be open on Sundays. Foreign money orders are paid out in German Marks.

12 stamps please
zwölf Briefmarken bitte
tsvoelf breef-mark-en bit-e

At the post office

Can I have a telegram form, please?
Könnte ich bitte einen Telegrammvordruck haben?
koent-e eekh bit-e yn-en tay-lay-gram-foar-drook hab-en

I need to send this by courier
Ich muß das per Kurier schicken
eekh moos das per koo-reer shik-en

I want to send a telegram
Ich möchte ein Telegramm schicken
eekh moekht-e yn tay-lay-gram shik-en

I want to send this by registered mail
Ich möchte das per Einschreiben schicken
eekh moekht-e das per yn-shryb-en shik-en

I want to send this parcel
Ich möchte dieses Paket abschicken
eekh moekht-e deez-es pa-kayt ap-shik-en

When will it arrive?
Wann wird es ankommen?
van virt es an-kom-en

How much is a letter — to Britain?
Wieviel kostet ein Brief — nach Großbritannien?
vee-feel kost-et yn breef — nakh groas-bri-tan-ee-en

— to the United States?
— in die Vereinigten Staaten
— in dee fer-yn-eeg-ten shtat-en

202

Can I have six stamps for postcards to Britain?
Kann ich bitte sechs Briefmarken für Postkarten nach
 Großbritannien haben?
*kan eekh bit-e zeks **breef**-mark-en für **post**-kart-en nakh
 gros-bri-**tan**-ee-en **hab**-en*

Using the telephone

After reunification, telephone links between east and west
had to be established, upgraded and new area codes intro-
duced or changed. This complex process is now complete.
You can make local and long-distance calls from all post offices and public call boxes. Most kiosks accept phone cards,
which are available at any post office. Phone boxes usually
have instructions in English and German and can be operated
with coins or cards, although the card phones are rapidly taking over. The ringing tone in Germany is a slowly repeating
tone rather than a double ring, while the engaged sound consists of quickly repeating tones.

Germany's country code is 49, so from Britain you dial
0049, then leave the initial 0 of the area code, dialling
straight through. To phone Britain from Germany dial 0044,
and similarly skip the 0 of the area code, dialling straight
through.

Can I use the telephone, please?
Kann ich bitte das Telefon benutzen?
*kan eekh bit-e das **tay**-lay-foan be-**noots**-en*

Using the telephone

Can you connect me with the international operator?
Könnten Sie mich bitte mit der internationalen Telefonver-
mittlung verbinden?
*koent-en zee meekh bit-e mit der in-ter-na-tsee-oa-nal-en
tay-lay-foan-fer-mit-loong fer-bind-en*

Can I dial direct?
Kann ich direkt wählen?
kan eekh dee-rekt vel-en

How do I use the telephone?
Wie verwendet man dieses Telefon?
vee fer-vend-et man deez-es tay-lay-foan

I must make a phone call to Britain
Ich muß mit Großbritannien telefonieren
eekh moos mit groas-bri-tan-ee-en tay-lay-fo-neer-en

I need to make a phone call
Ich muß telefonieren
eekh moos tay-lay-fo-neer-en

The number I need is...
Die Nummer, die ich brauche, lautet...
dee noom-er dee eekh browkh-e lowt-et...

How much is it to phone to London?
Wieviel kostet es nach London anzurufen?
vee-feel kost-et es nakh lon-don an-tsoo-roof-en

What you may hear

What is the charge?
Was kostet das?
vas kost-et das

Please, call me back
Bitte rufen Sie mich zurück
bit-e roof-en zee meekh tsoo-rûk

I am sorry. We were cut off
Es tut mir leid. Die Leitung wurde unterbrochen
es toot meer lyt dee lyt-oong voord-e oont-er-brokh-en

I would like to make a reversed charge call
Ich möchte gerne einen vom Empfänger bezahlten Anruf
  machen
*eekh moekht-e gern-e yn-en fom emp-feng-er be-tsalt-en
  an-roof makh-en*

What is the code for the UK?
Was ist die Vorwahl für Großbritannien?
vas ist dee foar-val fûr gros-bri-tan-ee-en

What you may hear

Bitte, tun Sie das
Please go ahead
bit-e toon zee das

Changing money

Die Leitung ist belegt
The line is engaged
dee **lyt**-oong ist be-**laygt**

Die Nummer funktioniert nicht
The number is out of order
dee **noom**-er foonk-tsee-o-**neert** neekht

Ich komme bei dieser Nummer nicht durch
I cannot obtain this number
eekh **kom**-e by deez-er **noom**-eer neekht **doorkh**

Ich stelle Sie an Herrn Smith durch
I am putting you through to Mr Smith
eekh **stel**-e zee an hern **smith** doorkh

Ich versuche, Sie zu verbinden
I am trying to connect you
eekh fer-**zookh**-e zee tsoo fer-**bind**-en

Changing money

Bank opening times are given under in Getting Around (*see* page 67). Bureaux de Change at airports and border crossings are usually open from 6am to 10pm. At border stations they open for all international trains.

Germany offers fewer opportunities to use credit cards

than most other western countries, as the Germans still prefer to use cash. It is a good idea to carry traveller's cheques
in case your credit cards are not accepted.

Can I contact my bank to arrange for a transfer?
Kann ich mich mit meiner Bank über die Regelung einer
    Überweisung in Verbindung setzen?
*kan eekh meekh mit myn-er **bank** ûb-er dee **rayg**-el-oong
    yn-er ûb-er-**vyz**-oong in fer-**bind**-oong zets-en*

**I would like to obtain a cash advance with my credit
    card**
Ich hätte gerne eine Bargeldauszahlung auf meine Kredit-
    karte
*eekh **het**-e gern-e yn-e **bar**-gelt-ows-tsal-oong owf myn-e
    kray-**deet**-kart-e*

Has my cash arrived?
Ist mein Geld angekommen?
*ist myn **gelt** an-ge-kom-en*

Here is my passport
Hier ist mein Paß
heer** ist myn **pas

I would like to cash a cheque with my Eurocheque card
Ich möchte gerne mit meiner Eurocheque-Karte einen
    Scheck einlösen
*eekh **moekht**-e gern-e mit myn-er **oy**-roa-shek-kart-e yn-en
    shek yn-loez-en*

Changing money

This is the name and address of my bank
Das sind Name und Adresse meiner Bank
*das zint **nam**-e oont a-**dres**-e myn-er **bank***

What is the rate of exchange?
Was ist der Wechselkurs?
***vas** ist der **veks**-el-koors*

What is your commission?
Wie hoch ist Ihre Kommission?
*vee **hoakh** ist eer-e ko-mee-see-**oan***

Can I change — these traveller's cheques?
Kann ich — diese Reiseschecks — hier umtauschen?
***kan** eekh — deez-e **ryz**-e-sheks — heer **oom**-towsh-en*

— **these notes?**
— diese Banknoten?
— *deez-e **bank**-noat-en*

What is the rate for — sterling?
Was ist der gängige Kurs für — britische Pfund?
*vas ist der **geng**-eeg-e- **koors** fûr — **brit**-eesh-e **pfoont***

— **dollars?**
— Dollars?
— ***dol**-ars*

208

HEALTH

Before you go

Nobody plans to fall sick while on holiday, but it can happen. If you are British, you should obtain an E111 form from a post office, which entitles you to medical treatment in other European Union countries. In addition to this, it is advisable to take out travel insurance. If you are not from an EU country, you should consider signing up with a medical-assistance company.

Hours and numbers

Surgery hours are generally from 10am to 12 noon and 4pm to 6pm, except for Wednesdays and the weekend. In an emergency, call 110 for accidents and emergencies or 112 for fire services. At the moment you are not required to be immunised before making your trip.

What's wrong?

I need a doctor
Ich brauche einen Arzt
*eekh **browkh**-e yn-en **artst***

What's wrong?

Can I see a doctor?
Kann ich einen Arzt sehen?
*kan eekh yn-en **artst** zay-en*

He has been badly injured
Er wurde schwer verletzt
*er voord-e **shvayr** fer-**letst***

He is unconscious
Er ist bewußtlos
*er ist be-**voost**-loas*

He has burnt himself
Er hat sich verbrannt
*er hat zeekh fer-**brant***

He has dislocated his shoulder
Er hat sich die Schulter verrenkt
*er hat zeekh dee **shoolt**-er fer-**renkt***

He is hurt
Er ist verletzt
*er ist fer-**letst***

My son is ill
Mein Sohn ist krank
*myn **zoan** ist **krank***

I am a diabetic
Ich bin Diabetiker
*eekh bin dee-a-**bay**-teek-er*

What's wrong?

I am allergic to penicillin
Ich bin gegen Penizillin allergisch
*eekh bin gayg-en pe-nee-tsee-**leen** a-**lerg**-eesh*

I am badly sunburnt
Ich habe einen starken Sonnenbrand
*eekh hab-e yn-en **shtark**-en **zon**-en-brant*

I am constipated
Ich habe Verstopfung
*eekh hab-e fer-**shtopf**-oong*

I cannot sleep
Ich kann nicht schlafen
*eekh kan neekht **shlaf**-en*

I feel dizzy
Ich fühle mich schwindelich
*eekh fûl-e meekh **shvinde**-leekh*

I feel faint
Ich fühle mich sehr schwach
*eekh fûl-e meekh zayr **shvakh***

I feel nauseous
Mir ist übel
*meer ist **ûb**-el*

I fell
Ich bin gefallen
*eekh bin ge-**fal**-en*

What's wrong?

I have a pain here
Ich habe hier Schmerzen
*eekh hab-e heer **shmerts**-en*

I have a rash here
Ich habe hier einen Ausschlag
*eekh hab-e heer yn-en **ows**-shlag*

I have been sick
Ich habe mich übergeben
*eekh hab-e meekh ûb-er-**gayb**-en*

I have been stung
Ich wurde gestochen
*eekh voord-e ge-**shtokh**-en*

I have cut myself
Ich habe mich geschnitten
*eekh hab-e meekh ge-**shnit**-en*

I have diarrhoea
Ich habe Durchfall
*eekh hab-e **doorkh**-fal*

I have pulled a muscle
Ich habe einen Muskel gezerrt
*eekh hab-e yn-en **moosk**-el ge-tsert*

I have sunstroke
Ich habe einen Sonnenstich
*eekh hab-e yn-en **zon**-en-shtikh*

What's wrong?

I suffer from high blood pressure
Ich leide an hohem Blutdruck
eekh lyd-e an hoa-em bloot-drook

I think I have food poisoning
Ich glaube ich habe eine Lebensmittelvergiftung
eekh glowb-e eekh hab-e yn-e layb-enz-mit-el-fer-gift-oong

It is inflamed here
Es ist hier entzündet
es ist heer ent-tsûnd-et

My arm is broken
Mein Arm ist gebrochen
myn arm ist ge-brokh-en

My stomach is upset
Ich habe einen verdorbenen Magen
eekh hab-e yn-en fer-dorb-en-en mag-en

My tongue is coated
Meine Zunge ist belegt
myn-e tsoong-e ist be-laygt

She has a temperature
Sie hat erhöhte Temperatur
zee hat er-hoe-te tem-pe-ra-toor

She has been bitten
Sie wurde gebissen
zee voord-e ge-bis-en

What's wrong?

She has sprained her ankle
Sie hat sich den Knöchel verstaucht
*zee hat zeekh den **knoekh**-el fer-**shtowkht***

There is a swelling here
Da ist es geschwollen
*da ist es ge-**shvol**-en*

I have hurt — my arm
   Ich habe — meinen Arm verletzt
*eekh hab-e — myn-en **arm** fer-**letst***

      — my leg
      — mein Bein verletzt
      *— myn **byn** fer-**letst***

      It is painful — to walk
Ich habe Schmerzen beim — Gehen
*eekh hab-e **shmerts**-en bym — **gay**-en*

      — to breathe
      — Atmen
      *— **at**-men*

      — to swallow
      — Schlucken
      *— **shlook**-en*

I have — a headache
   Ich habe — Kopfschmerzen
*eekh hab-e — **kopf**-shmerts-en*

What's wrong?

— **a sore throat**
— Halsschmerzen
— *hals-shmerts-en*

— **earache**
— Ohrenschmerzen
— *oar-en-shmerts-en*

— **cramp**
— einen Krampf
— *yn-en krampf*

I am taking these drugs

Ich nehme diese Medikamente
eekh naym-e deez-e may-dee-ka-ment-e

Can you give me a prescription for them?

Können Sie mir ein Rezept dafür geben?
koen-en zee meer yn re-tsept da-für gayb-en

Do I have to go into hospital?

Muß ich ins Krankenhaus gehen?
moos eekh ins krank-en-hows gay-en

Do I need an operation?

Brauche ich eine Operation?
browkh-e eekh yn-e o-pe-ra-tsee-oan

I am ill

Ich bin krank
eekh bin krank

At the hospital

I am on the pill
Ich nehme die Pille
eekh naym-e dee pil-e

I am pregnant
Ich bin schwanger
eekh bin shvang-er

My blood group is . . .
Meine Blutgruppe ist . . .
myn-e bloot-groop-e ist . . .

I do not know my blood group
Ich kenne meine Blutgruppe nicht
eekh ken-e myn-e bloot-groop-e neekht

At the hospital

Here is my E111 form
Hier ist mein E111
heer ist myn ay-hoond-ert-elf

How do I get reimbursed?
Wie bekomme ich die Kosten zurückerstattet?
vee be-kom-e eekh dee kost-en tsoo-rûk-er-shtat-et

Must I stay in bed?
Muß ich im Bett bleiben?
moos eekh im bet blyb-en

When will I be able to travel?
Wann werde ich in der Lage sein, zu reisen?
van vayrd-e eekh in der lag-e zyn tsoo ryz-en

Will I be able to go out tomorrow?
Werde ich morgen das Haus verlassen können?
vayrd-e eekh morg-en das hows ver-lass-en koen-en

Parts of the body

ankle
Fußgelenk
foos-ge-lenk

cheek
Wange
vang-e

arm
Arm
arm

chest
Brust
broost

back
Rücken
rûk-en

ear
Ohr
oar

bone
Knochen
knokh-en

elbow
Ellbogen
el-boag-en

breast
Brust
broost

eye
Auge
owg-e

217

Parts of the body

face
Gesicht
ge-zeekht

finger
Finger
fing-er

foot
Fuß
foos

hand
Hand
hant

heart
Herz
herts

kidney
Niere
neer-e

knee
Knie
knee

leg
Bein
byn

liver
Leber
layb-er

lungs
Lunge
loong-e

mouth
Mund
moont

muscle
Muskel
moosk-el

neck
Hals
hals

nose
Nase
naz-e

skin
Haut
howt

stomach
Magen
mag-en

throat
Hals
hals

wrist
Handgelenk
hant-ge-lenk

At the dentist's

I have toothache
Ich habe Zahnschmerzen
eekh hab-e tsan-shmerts-en

I have broken a tooth
Ich habe einen zerbrochenen Zahn
eekh hab-e yn-en tser-brokh-en-en tsan

I have to see the dentist
Ich muß zum Zahnarzt gehen
eekh moos tsoom tsan-artst gay-en

My false teeth are broken
Meine dritten Zähne sind kaputt
myn-e drit-en tsen-e zint ka-poot

Can you repair them?
Können Sie sie reparieren?
koen-en zee zee re-ar-reer-en

My gums are sore
Mein Zahnfleisch ist entzündet
myn tsan-flysh ist ent-tsûnd-et

At the dentist's

Please give me an injection
Geben Sie mir bitte eine Spritze
gayb-en zee meer bit-e yn-e shprits-e

That hurts
Das tut weh
das toot vay

The filling has come out
Die Plombe ist herausgefallen
dee blomb-e ist hayr-ows-ge-fal-en

This one hurts
Der tut weh
dayr toot vay

Are you going to fill it?
Werden Sie ihn füllen?
vayrd-en zee een fûl-en

FOR YOUR INFORMATION

Numbers, etc

Cardinal numbers

0	null	*nool*
1	eins	*yns*
2	zwei	*tsvy*
3	drei	*dry*
4	vier	*feer*
5	fünf	*fûnf*
6	sechs	*zeks*
7	sieben	***zeeb-en***
8	acht	*akht*
9	neun	*noyn*
10	zehn	*tsayn*
11	elf	*elf*
12	zwölf	*tsvoelf*
13	dreizehn	***dry-tsayn***
14	vierzehn	***feer-tsayn***

Cardinal numbers

15	fünfzehn	*fûnf*-tsayn
16	sechzehn	*zekhs*-tsayn
17	siebzehn	*zeeb*-tsayn
18	achtzehn	*akht*-tsayn
19	neunzehn	*noyn*-stayn
20	zwanzig	*tsvan*-tseekh
21	einundzwanzig	*yn*-oont-tsvan-tseekh
22	zweiundzwanzig	*tsvy*-oont-tsvan-tseekh
23	dreiundzwanzig	*dry*-oont-tsvan-tseekh
24	vierundzwanzig	*feer*-oont-tsvan-steekh
25	fünfundzwanzig	*fûnf*-oont-tsvan-tseekh
26	sechsundzwanzig	*zeks*-oont-tsvan-tseekh
27	siebenundzwanzig	*zeeb*-en-oont-tsvan-steekh
28	achtundzwanzig	*akht*-oont-tsvan-tseekh
29	neunundzwanzig	*noyn*-oont-tsvan-tseekh
30	dreißig	*dry*-seekh
40	vierzig	*feer*-tseekh
50	fünfzig	*fûnf*-tseekh
60	sechzig	*zekh*-tseekh
70	siebzig	*zeeb*-tseekh

Ordinal numbers

80	achtzig	*akh-tseekh*
90	neunzig	*noyn-tseekh*
100	hundert	*hoond-ert*
200	zweihundert	*tsvy-hoond-ert*
300	dreihundert	*dry-hoond-ert*
400	vierhundert	*feer-hoond-ert*
500	fünfhundert	*fûnf-hoond-ert*
600	sechshundert	*zeks-hoond-ert*
700	siebenhundert	*zeeb-en-hoond-ert*
800	achthundert	*akht-hoond-ert*
900	neunhundert	*noyn-hoond-ert*
1000	tausend	*towz-ent*
2000	zweitausend	*tsvy-towz-ent*
3000	dreitausen	*dry-towz-ent*
4000	viertausend	*feer-towz-ent*
1000000	eine Million	*yn-e mee-lee-oan*

Ordinal numbers

1st	erster	*erst-er*
2nd	zweiter	*tsvyt-er*

Fractions and percentages

3rd	dritter	**drit**-er
4th	vierter	**feert**-er
5th	fünfter	**fûnft**-er
xth	xter	**xt**-er

Fractions and percentages

a half	ein halb	yn **halp**
a quarter	ein Viertel	yn **feert**-el
a third	ein Drittel	yn **drit**-el
two thirds	zwei Drittel	tsvy **drit**-el
10 per cent	zehn Prozent	tsayn pro-**tsent**

Time

Days

Sunday	Sonntag *zon-tag*
Monday	Montag *moan-tag*
Tuesday	Dienstag *deens-tag*
Wednesday	Mittwoch *mit-vokh*
Thursday	Donnerstag *don-ers-tag*
Friday	Freitag *fry-tag*
Saturday	Samstag *zams-tag*

Dates

on Friday	am Freitag *am fry-tag*
next Tuesday	nächsten Dienstag *nekst-en deens-tag*
last Tuesday	letzten Dienstag *letst-en deens-tag*
yesterday	gestern *gest-ern*
today	heute *hoyt-e*
tomorrow	morgen *morg-en*
in June	im Juni *im yoon-ee*
7th July	siebter Juli *zeept-er yool-ee*

The seasons

| **next week** | nächste Woche *nekst-e **vokh**-e* |
| **last month** | letzten Monat *letst-en **moa**-nat* |

The Seasons

spring	Frühjahr *frû-yar*
summer	Sommer *zom-er*
autumn	Herbst *herpst*
winter	Winter *vint-er*

Times of the year

in spring	im Frühjahr *im frû-yar*
in summer	im Sommer *im zom-er*
in autumn	im Herbst *im herpst*
in winter	im Winter *im vint-er*

Months

January	Januar *ya-noo-ar*
February	Februar *fayb-roo-ar*
March	März *merts*
April	April *a-preel*
May	Mai *my*
June	Juni *yoon-ee*

July	Juli *yool-ee*
August	August *ow-goost*
September	September *zep-temb-er*
October	Oktober *ok-toab-er*
November	November *noa-vemb-er*
December	Dezember *day-tsemb-er*

Public holidays

The following holidays are observed in Germany:

1 January, New Year's Day
Neujahr
noy-yar

6 January, Twelfth Night (Bavaria and Baden
 Württemberg only)
Heilige Dreikönige/Epiphania
hyl-eege dry-koen-eege

Good Friday
Karfreitag
kar-fry-tag

Easter Sunday
Ostersonntag

227

Public holidays

*oast-er-**zon**-tag*

Easter Monday
Ostermontag
*oast-er-**moan**-tag*

1 May, May Day
Maifeiertag/Tag der Arbeit
***my**-fy-er-tag*

Ascension
(Christi) Himmelfahrt
***krist**-ee **him**-el-fart*

Whit Sunday
Pfingstsonntag
*pfingst-**zon**-tag*

Whit Monday / Pentecost
Pfingstmontag
*pfingst-**moan**-tag*

Corpus Christi (southern Germany only)
Fronleichnam
*fron-**lykh**-nam*

Feast of the Assumption
Mariä Himmelfahrt (Bavaria and Saarland only)
*ma-**ree**-e **him**-el-fart*

3 October, German unification
Tag der Einheit
tag der yn-hyt

1 November, All Saints' Day
Allerheiligen
al-er-hyl-eeg-en

24 December, Christmas Eve
Heilig Abend (shops closed in afternoon)
hyl-eekh a-bent

25 December, Christmas Day
erster Weihnachtsfeiertag
erst-er vy-nakhts-fy-er-tag

26 December, Boxing Day
zweiter Weihnachtsfeiertag
tsvyt-er vy-nakhts-fy-er-tag

31 December, New Year's Eve
Sylvester
zil-vest-er

Colours

beige
beige
bayzh

black
schwarz
shvarts

blue
blau
blow

brown
braun
brown

cream
cremefarben
kraym-farb-en

fawn
khaki
ka-kee

gold
golden
gold-en

green
grün
grûn

grey
grau
grow

mauve
violett
vee-oa-let

orange
orange
o-ranzh-e

pink
rosa
roaz-a

purple
lila
lee-la

red
rot
roat

silver
silbern
zilb-ern

white
weiß
vys

tan
gelbbraun
gelp-brown

yellow
gelb
gelp

Common adjectives

bad
schlecht
shlekht

expensive
teuer
toy-er

beautiful
schön
shoen

difficult
schwierig
shveer-eekh

big
groß
groas

easy
leicht
lykht

cheap
billig
beel-eekh

fast
schnell
shnel

cold
kalt
kalt

good
gut
goot

Common adjectives

high
hoch
hoakh

old
alt
alt

hot
heiß
hys

short
kurz
koorts

little
wenig
vayn-eekh

slow
langsam
lang-zam

long
lang
lang

small
klein
klyn

new
neu
noy

ugly
häßlich
hes-leekh

Signs and notices

These are some of the signs and notices you may see in Germany. *See also* Road signs, page 114.

Achtung
akh-toong
caution

besetzt
be-zetst
occupied

Aufzug
owf-tsoog
lift / elevator

nicht auf das Gras gehen
*neekht owf das **gras** gay-en*
keep off the grass

Ausgang
ows-gang
exit

bitte klingeln
*bit-e **kling**-eln*
please ring

Information
*in-for-ma-tsee-**oan***
information

drücken
drük-en
push

Ausverkauf
ows-fer-kowf
sale

Eingang
yn-gang
entrance

Verkauft
fer-kowft
sold out

Eintritt frei
*yn-trit **fry***
no admission charge

Signs and notices

Telefon
tay-lay-foan
telephone

Feuerwehr
foy-er-vayr
fire brigade

frei
fry
vacant

Fundamt
foont-amt
Lost Property Office

Betreten verboten
be-trayt-en fer-boat-en
No trespassing

Gefahr
ge-far
danger

geschlossen
ge-shlos-en
closed

Gift
gift
poison

heiß
hys
hot

kalt
kalt
cold

Kasse
kas-e
cashier

Durchfahrt verboten
doorkh-fart fer-boat-en
no thoroughfare

kein Eingang
kyn yn-gang
no entry

Krankenhaus
krank-en-hows
hospital

Sanitäter
zan-ee-tet-er
ambulance

Lebensgefahr
layb-ens-ge-far
danger of death

234

Nachmittags geschlossen
nakh-mit-ags-ge-shlos-en
closed in the afternoon

nicht berühren
neekht be-rûr-en
do not touch

nicht nach außen lehnen
neekht nakh ows-en layn-en
do not lean out

Rauchen verboten
rowkh-en fer-boat-en
no smoking

Notausgang
noat-ows-gang
emergency exit

private Zufahrt
pree-vat-e tsoo-fart
private road

Radweg
rat-vayg
cycle path

Raucherabteil
rowkh-er-ap-tyl
smoking compartment

Geschäftsauflösung
ge-shefts-owf-loez-oong
closing down sale

bitte rechts fahren
bit-e rekhts far-en
keep to the right

Andenken
an-denk-en
souvenirs

Reiseagentur
ryz-e-a-gen-toor
travel agency

Sonderangebot
zond-er-an-ge-boat
special offer

Trinkwasser
trink-vas-er
drinking water

Umleitung
oom-lyt-oong
diversion

ziehen
tsee-en
pull

Signs and notices

zu verkaufen
tsoo-fer-kowf-en
for sale

zu mieten
tsoo meet-en
to let/for hire

Preisliste
prys-list-e
price list

willkommen
vil-kom-en
welcome

Gepäck
ge-pek
baggage

Bank
bank
bank

Zoll
tsol
Customs

Notfall
noat-fal
Emergency

Feuermelder
foy-er-meld-er
fire alarm

reserviert
re-zer-veert
reserved

Raucherbereich
rowkh-er-be-rykh
smoking area

nur für . . . erlaubt
noor fûr . . . er-lowpt
allowed only for . . .

Achtung vor dem Hund
akh-toong foar dem hoont
beware of the dog

Polizei
po-lee-tsy
police

Feuergefahr
foy-er-ge-far
danger of fire

Nur für Mitarbeiter
noor fûr mit-ar-byt-er
employees only

Abfahrt / Abflüge
ap-fart / ap-flug-e
departures

Abfall
ap-fal
litter

offen
of-en
open

klingeln
kling-eln
ring

Ankunft
an-koonft
arrivals

Schule
shool-e
school

Eingang
yn-gang
entrance

Zeitplan
tstyt-plan
timetable

Herren
her-en
gentlemen

Damen
dam-en
ladies

Fotografieren verboten
foa-toa-gra-feer-en fer-boat-en
no picture taking

Notbremse
noat-bremz-e
communication cord (rail)

nur zur äußerlichen Anwendung
*noor tsoor **oys**-er-leekh-en **an**-vend-oong*
for external use only

Signs and notices

Es ist verboten, während der Fahrt mit dem Fahrer zu sprechen

*es ist fer-**boat**-en ver-ent der **fart** mit dem far-er tsoo **shprekh**-en*

It is forbidden to speak to the driver while the bus is moving

eintreten, ohne zu klopfen

*yn-trayt-en oan-e tsoo **klopf**-en*

enter without knocking

IN AN EMERGENCY

What to do

The German police force is called Polizei and officers are dressed in green uniforms with white caps, while their patrol cars are also green and white. Police officers should be approached with due respect and most of them do not speak more than basic English.

If you witness an accident or criminal activity, you should phone the emergency services on 110. The call is free from anywhere, including public phone boxes. You will also find clearly marked emergency phones (*Notruf*) in railway stations and on main roads and motorways.

In the case of fire, the fire-fighting services can be reached by dialling 112 free of charge.

Each town and city has its own medical emergency service organised to offer assistance night and day. You will find the phone number in the local telephone directory. Chemist shops also have a night and Sunday service, and in each chemist shop you will find the address of the nearest duty chemist.

Embassies will provide lists of doctors or pertinent legal advice, and can also contact your relatives in an emergency. Consulates can be found in major cities.

What to do

Call — the fire brigade
Rufen — Sie die Feuerwehr
roof-en — zee dee foy-er-vayr

— the police
— Sie die Polizei
— zee dee po-lee-tsy

— an ambulance
— Sie die Sanitäter
— zee dee zan-ee-tet-er

Get a doctor
Holen Sie einen Arzt
hoal-en zee yn-en artst

There is a fire
Es brennt
es brent

Where is — the police station?
Wo ist — die Polizeiwache?
voa ist — dee po-lee-tsy-vakh-e

— the British consulate?
— das britische Konsulat?
— das bri-tish-e koan-soo-lat